Cupcakes

igloobooks

igloobooks

*Published in 2014
by Igloo Books Ltd
Cottage Farm
Sywell
Northants
NN6 0BJ
www.igloobooks.com*

The measurements used are approximate.

Food photography and recipe development: PhotoCuisine UK

*GUA006 0714
2 4 6 8 10 9 7 5 3 1
ISBN: 978-1-78440-296-9*

Printed and manufactured in China

Contents

Basic Cupcakes

Preparation time: **45 minutes** | Cooking time: **10–15 minutes** | Makes: **12**

Ingredients:

110 g / 4 oz / ⅔ cup self-raising flour, sifted
110 g / 4 oz / ½ cup caster (superfine) sugar
110 g / 4 oz / ½ cup butter, softened
2 large eggs
1 tsp vanilla extract

To decorate:

100 g / 3 ½ oz / ½ cup butter, softened
200 g / 7 oz / 2 cups icing (confectioners') sugar
2 tbsp cocoa powder
2 tsp instant espresso powder
white and dark chocolate vermicelli to sprinkle

Mocha swirl cupcakes

Method

STEP 1
Preheat the oven to 190°C (170°C fan) / 375F / gas 5 and line a 12-hole cupcake tin with paper cases.

STEP 2
Combine the flour, sugar, butter, eggs and vanilla extract in a bowl and whisk together for 2 minutes or until smooth.

STEP 3
Divide the mixture between the cases, then transfer the tin to the oven and bake for 10–15 minutes. Test with a wooden toothpick, if it comes out clean, the cakes are done. Transfer the cakes to a wire rack and leave to cool completely.

STEP 4
Beat the butter until smooth, then gradually whisk in the icing sugar, cocoa and espresso powder.

STEP 5
Spoon the mixture into a piping bag fitted with a large star nozzle and pipe a swirl of icing on top of each cake. Sprinkle with chocolate vermicelli.

Preparation time: **45 minutes** | Cooking time: **10–15 minutes** | Makes: **12**

Ingredients:

110 g / 4 oz / ⅔ cup self-raising flour, sifted
110 g / 4 oz / ½ cup caster (superfine) sugar
110 g / 4 oz / ½ cup butter, softened
1 tsp vanilla extract
2 large eggs
150 g / 5 ½ oz / 1 cup blueberries

To decorate:

400 ml / 14 fl. oz / 1 ⅔ cups double (heavy) cream
36 blueberries

Blueberry cream cupcakes

Method

STEP 1
Preheat the oven to 190°C (170°C fan) / 375F / gas 5 and line a 12-hole cupcake tin with paper cases.

STEP 2
Whisk together the flour, sugar, butter, vanilla extract and eggs in a bowl until smooth and light. Fold in the blueberries. Divide the mixture between the paper cases, then transfer the tin to the oven and bake for 10–15 minutes.

STEP 3
Test the cakes with a toothpick; if it comes out clean, the cakes are done. Transfer the cakes to a wire rack and leave to cool completely.

STEP 4
Whip the cream until it holds its shape, then spoon it onto the cakes and top with the blueberries.

Preparation time: **40 minutes** | Cooking time: **10–15 minutes** | Makes: **12**

Ingredients:

110 g / 4 oz / ⅔ cup self-raising flour, sifted
110 g / 4 oz / ½ cup caster (superfine) sugar
110 g / 4 oz / ½ cup butter, softened
2 large eggs
1 lemon, zest finely grated
1 tbsp poppy seeds

To decorate:

110 g / 4 oz / ½ cup butter, softened
225 g / 8 oz / 2 ¼ cups icing (confectioners') sugar
1 tbsp lemon juice
2 tbsp poppy seeds

Lemon and poppy seed cupcakes

Method

STEP 1
Preheat the oven to 190°C (170°C fan) / 375F / gas 5 and line a 12-hole cupcake tin with paper cases.

STEP 2
Combine the flour, sugar, butter, eggs, lemon zest and poppy seeds in a bowl and whisk together for 2 minutes or until smooth.

STEP 3
Divide the mixture between the cake cases then transfer the tin to the oven and bake for 10–15 minutes. Test with a wooden toothpick, if it comes out clean, the cakes are done. Transfer the cakes to a wire rack and leave to cool completely.

STEP 4
To make the buttercream, beat the butter until smooth then beat in the icing sugar. Use a whisk to incorporate the lemon juice, then whisk for 2 minutes or until well whipped.

STEP 5
Spoon the buttercream into a piping bag fitted with a large star nozzle and pipe a swirl on top of each cake. Finish with a sprinkle of poppy seeds.

Preparation time: **45 minutes** | Cooking time: **10–15 minutes** | Makes: **12**

Ingredients:

110 g / 4 oz / ⅔ cup self-raising flour, sifted
110 g / 4 oz / ½ cup caster (superfine) sugar
110 g / 4 oz / ½ cup butter, softened
2 large eggs
2 tbsp malted milk powder

To decorate:

100 g / 3 ½ oz / ½ cup butter, softened
200 g / 7 oz / 2 cups icing (confectioners') sugar
1 tbsp instant malted milk powder
36 chocolate balls

Malted milk cupcakes

Method

STEP 1
Preheat the oven to 190°C (170°C fan) / 375F / gas 5 and line a 12-hole cupcake tin with paper cases.

STEP 2
Combine the flour, sugar, butter, eggs and malted milk powder in a bowl and whisk together for 2 minutes or until smooth.

STEP 3
Divide the mixture between the cases, then transfer the tin to the oven and bake for 10–15 minutes. Test with a wooden toothpick, if it comes out clean, the cakes are done. Transfer the cakes to a wire rack and leave to cool completely.

STEP 4
Beat the butter until smooth, then gradually whisk in the icing sugar and malted milk powder.

STEP 5
Spoon the mixture into a piping bag, fitted with a large star nozzle, and pipe a swirl of icing on top of each cake. Top each cake with 3 chocolate balls.

Preparation time: 45 minutes | **Cooking time:** 10–15 minutes | **Makes:** 12

Ingredients:

110 g / 4 oz / ⅔ cup self-raising flour, sifted
110 g / 4 oz / ½ cup caster (superfine) sugar
110 g / 4 oz / ½ cup butter, softened
2 large eggs
2 tbsp unsweetened cocoa powder

To decorate:

100 g / 3 ½ oz / ½ cup butter, softened
200 g / 7 oz / 2 cups icing (confectioners') sugar
2 tbsp cocoa powder
double-sided white and dark chocolate hearts

Chocolate heart cupcakes

Method

STEP 1
Preheat the oven to 190°C (170°C fan) / 375F / gas 5 and line a 12-hole cupcake tin with paper cases.

STEP 2
Combine the flour, sugar, butter, eggs and cocoa in a bowl and whisk together for 2 minutes or until smooth.

STEP 3
Divide the mixture between the cases, then transfer the tin to the oven and bake for 10–15 minutes. Test with a wooden toothpick, if it comes out clean, the cakes are done. Transfer the cakes to a wire rack and leave to cool completely.

STEP 4
Beat the butter until smooth, then gradually whisk in the icing sugar and cocoa powder.

STEP 5
Spoon the buttercream into a piping bag fitted with a large star nozzle and pipe a swirl onto each cake. Decorate with chocolate hearts.

Preparation time: 1 hour | **Cooking time: 10–15 minutes** | **Makes: 12**

Ingredients:

110 g / 4 oz / ⅔ cup self-raising flour, sifted
110 g / 4 oz / ½ cup caster (superfine) sugar
110 g / 4 oz / ½ cup butter, softened
2 large eggs
1 tsp vanilla extract

To decorate:

200 g / 7 oz / ⅔ cup ready-to-roll fondant icing
150 g / 5 ½ oz / 1 ½ cups icing (confectioners') sugar
hundreds and thousands and edible glitter

Fondant sprinkle cupcakes

Method

STEP 1
Preheat the oven to 190°C (170°C fan) / 375F / gas 5 and line a 12-hole cupcake tin with paper cases.

STEP 2
Combine the flour, sugar, butter, eggs and vanilla extract in a bowl and whisk together for 2 minutes or until smooth. Divide the mixture between the cases, then transfer the tin to the oven and bake for 10–15 minutes.

STEP 3
Test with a wooden toothpick, if it comes out clean, the cakes are done. Transfer the cakes to a wire rack and leave to cool completely.

STEP 4
Roll out the fondant icing, then cut out 12 circles a little smaller in diameter than the top of the cakes. Wet the backs with a dab of water, then smooth them onto the cakes.

STEP 5
Add a little water to the icing sugar, a few drops at a time, until it forms a smooth, spreadable icing. Spoon a little onto each cake, spreading it out into a circle with the back of the spoon.

STEP 6
Pour some hundreds and thousands onto a plate, then dip the top of each cake to fully coat the glacé icing. Finish with a sprinkle of edible glitter.

Preparation time: 40 minutes | **Cooking time: 10–15 minutes** | **Makes: 12**

Ingredients:

110 g / 4 oz / ⅔ cup self-raising flour, sifted
110 g / 4 oz / ½ cup caster (superfine) sugar
110 g / 4 oz / ½ cup butter, softened
2 large eggs
1 tsp rosewater

To decorate:

110 g / 4 oz / ½ cup butter, softened
225 g / 8 oz / 2 ¼ cups icing (confectioners') sugar
2 tbsp milk
1 tsp rosewater
12 sugar flowers and leaves

Rose buttercream cupcakes

Method

STEP 1
Preheat the oven to 190°C (170°C fan) / 375F / gas 5 and line a 12-hole cupcake tin with paper cases.

STEP 2
Combine the flour, sugar, butter, eggs and rosewater in a bowl and whisk together for 2 minutes or until smooth.

STEP 3
Divide the mixture between the cake cases then transfer the tin to the oven and bake for 10–15 minutes. Test with a wooden toothpick, if it comes out clean, the cakes are done. Transfer the cakes to a wire rack and leave to cool completely.

STEP 4
To make the buttercream, beat the butter until smooth then beat in the icing sugar. Use a whisk to incorporate the milk and rosewater, then whisk for 2 minutes or until well whipped.

STEP 5
Spoon the icing into a piping bag fitted with a large star nozzle and pipe a big swirl on top of each cake. Decorate with the sugar flowers and leaves.

Preparation time: 40 minutes | Cooking time: 10–15 minutes | Makes: 12

Ingredients:

110 g / 4 oz / ⅔ cup self-raising flour, sifted
110 g / 4 oz / ½ cup caster (superfine) sugar
110 g / 4 oz / ½ cup butter, softened
2 large eggs
1 lemon, zest finely grated

To decorate:

110 g / 4 oz / ½ cup butter, softened
225 g / 8 oz / 2 ¼ cups icing (confectioners') sugar
1 tbsp lemon juice
100 g / 3 ½ oz / ⅓ cup yellow ready-to-roll fondant icing

Lemon rose cupcakes

Method

STEP 1
Preheat the oven to 190°C (170°C fan) / 375F / gas 5 and line a 12-hole cupcake tin with paper cases.

STEP 2
Combine the flour, sugar, butter, eggs and lemon zest in a bowl and whisk together for 2 minutes or until smooth.

STEP 3
Divide the mixture between the cake cases then transfer the tin to the oven and bake for 10–15 minutes. Test with a wooden toothpick, if it comes out clean, the cakes are done. Transfer the cakes to a wire rack and leave to cool completely.

STEP 4
To make the buttercream, beat the butter until smooth then beat in the icing sugar. Use a whisk to incorporate the lemon juice, then whisk for 2 minutes or until well whipped.

STEP 5
Spoon the icing into a piping bag fitted with a large star nozzle and pipe a swirl on top of each cake.

STEP 6
Roll out the yellow fondant and cut it into 12 ribbons. Roll each ribbon up into a rose and position them on top of the cakes. Finish with a light dusting of icing sugar.

Preparation time: **1 hour 10 minutes** | Cooking time: **10–15 minutes** | Makes: **12**

Ingredients:

110 g / 4 oz / ⅔ cup self-raising flour, sifted
110 g / 4 oz / ½ cup caster (superfine) sugar
110 g / 4 oz / ½ cup butter, softened
2 large eggs
1 tsp vanilla extract

To decorate:

300 g / 10 ½ oz / 1 cup ready-to-roll fondant icing
blue food colouring

Fondant stripe cupcakes

Method

STEP 1
Preheat the oven to 190°C (170°C fan) / 375F / gas 5 and line a 12-hole cupcake tin with paper cases.

STEP 2
Combine the flour, sugar, butter, eggs and vanilla extract in a bowl and whisk together for 2 minutes or until smooth. Divide the mixture between the cases, then transfer the tin to the oven and bake for 10–15 minutes.

STEP 3
Test with a wooden toothpick, if it comes out clean, the cakes are done. Transfer the cakes to a wire rack and leave to cool completely.

STEP 4
Colour half of the fondant icing pale blue and roll out both pieces. Cut 6 circles out of each colour, then stack a blue circle on top of each white circle and cut into strips. Use alternating coloured stripes to make up 12 circles, then attach to the top of the cakes with a dab of water.

Preparation time: **40 minutes** | Cooking time: **10–15 minutes** | Makes: **12**

Ingredients:
110 g / 4 oz / ⅔ cup self-raising flour, sifted
110 g / 4 oz / ½ cup caster (superfine) sugar
110 g / 4 oz / ½ cup butter, softened
2 large eggs
1 tsp vanilla extract

To decorate:
110 g / 4 oz / ½ cup butter, softened
225 g / 8 oz / 2 ¼ cups icing (confectioners') sugar, plus extra for dusting
2 tbsp raspberry syrup
12 pink sweets

Raspberry buttercream cupcakes

Method

STEP 1
Preheat the oven to 190°C (170°C fan) / 375F / gas 5 and line a 12-hole cupcake tin with paper cases.

STEP 2
Combine the flour, sugar, butter, eggs and vanilla extract in a bowl and whisk together for 2 minutes or until smooth.

STEP 3
Divide the mixture between the cake cases then transfer the tin to the oven and bake for 10–15 minutes. Test with a wooden toothpick, if it comes out clean, the cakes are done. Transfer the cakes to a wire rack and leave to cool completely.

STEP 4
To make the buttercream, beat the butter until smooth then beat in the icing sugar. Use a whisk to incorporate the raspberry syrup, then whisk for 2 minutes or until well whipped.

STEP 5
Spoon the icing into a piping bag fitted with a large star nozzle and pipe a swirl on top of each cake. Finish with a pink sweet and a dusting of icing sugar.

Preparation time: **1 hour 20 minutes** | Cooking time: **10–15 minutes** | Makes: **12**

Ingredients:

110 g / 4 oz / ⅔ cup self-raising flour, sifted
110 g / 4 oz / ½ cup caster (superfine) sugar
110 g / 4 oz / ½ cup butter, softened
2 large eggs
1 tsp vanilla extract
75 g / 2 ½ oz / ½ cup white chocolate chips

To decorate:

3 x 100 g / 3 ½ oz / ⅔ cup bars of white chocolate
200 ml / 7 fl. oz / ¾ cup double (heavy) cream

White chocolate curl cupcakes

Method

STEP 1
Preheat the oven to 190°C (170°C fan) / 375F / gas 5 and line a 12-hole cupcake tin with paper cases.

STEP 2
Combine the flour, sugar, butter, eggs and vanilla extract in a bowl and whisk together for 2 minutes or until smooth. Fold in the chocolate chips, then divide the mixture between the paper cases.

STEP 3
Transfer the tin to the oven and bake for 10–15 minutes. Test with a wooden toothpick, if it comes out clean, the cakes are done. Transfer the cakes to a wire rack and leave to cool completely.

STEP 4
Finely chop 2 bars of the chocolate and transfer it to a mixing bowl. Heat the cream until it starts to simmer, then pour it over the chocolate and leave to stand for 30 seconds. Slowly stir the chocolate and cream together until it forms a smooth ganache.

STEP 5
Leave the ganache to cool until it's thick enough to hold its shape, then spread it over the cakes. Unwrap the third bar of white chocolate and warm one edge of it with your hand. Use a vegetable peeler to shave the chocolate into curls and arrange them on top of the cakes.

Preparation time: 50 minutes | **Cooking time: 10–15 minutes** | **Makes: 12**

Ingredients:

110 g / 4 oz / ⅔ cup self-raising flour, sifted
110 g / 4 oz / ½ cup caster (superfine) sugar
110 g / 4 oz / ½ cup butter, softened
2 large eggs
2 tbsp unsweetened cocoa powder
75 g / 2 ½ oz / ½ cup butterscotch pieces

To decorate:

100 g / 3 ½ oz / ½ cup butter, softened
200 g / 7 oz / 2 cups icing (confectioners') sugar
2 tbsp butterscotch syrup
white chocolate for grating
icing (confectioners') sugar and cocoa powder for dusting

Butterscotch cupcakes

Method

STEP 1
Preheat the oven to 190°C (170°C fan) / 375F / gas 5 and line a 12-hole cupcake tin with paper cases.

STEP 2
Combine the flour, sugar, butter, eggs, cocoa and butterscotch pieces in a bowl and whisk together for 2 minutes or until smooth.

STEP 3
Divide the mixture between the cases, then transfer the tin to the oven and bake for 10–15 minutes. Test with a wooden toothpick, if it comes out clean, the cakes are done. Transfer the cakes to a wire rack and leave to cool completely.

STEP 4
Beat the butter until smooth, then gradually whisk in the icing sugar and butterscotch syrup.

STEP 5
Spoon the mixture into a piping bag, fitted with a large star nozzle, and pipe a swirl of icing on top of each cake. Grate over a little white chocolate, then dust lightly with cocoa powder and icing sugar to finish.

Preparation time: 45 minutes | **Cooking time:** 10–15 minutes | **Makes:** 12

Ingredients:

110 g / 4 oz / ⅔ cup self-raising flour, sifted
110 g / 4 oz / ½ cup caster (superfine) sugar
110 g / 4 oz / ½ cup butter, softened
2 large eggs
1 tsp vanilla extract
2 tbsp freeze-dried strawberry pieces

To decorate:

110 g / 4 oz / ½ cup butter, softened
225 g / 8 oz / 2 ¼ cups icing (confectioners') sugar, plus extra for dusting
2 tbsp milk
1 tsp vanilla extract
3 tbsp freeze-dried strawberry pieces

Dried strawberry cupcakes

Method

STEP 1
Preheat the oven to 190°C (170°C fan) / 375F / gas 5 and line a 12-hole cupcake tin with paper cases.

STEP 2
Combine the flour, sugar, butter, eggs and vanilla extract in a bowl and whisk together for 2 minutes or until smooth.

STEP 3
Fold in the freeze-dried strawberries, then divide the mixture between the cake cases and bake for 10–15 minutes. Test with a wooden toothpick, if it comes out clean, the cakes are done. Transfer the cakes to a wire rack and leave to cool completely.

STEP 4
To make the buttercream, beat the butter until smooth then beat in the icing sugar. Use a whisk to incorporate the milk and vanilla extract, then whisk for 2 minutes or until well whipped. Finely chop 2 tbsp of the strawberry pieces and fold them into the buttercream.

STEP 5
Spread the buttercream over the cakes and top with the remaining strawberry pieces.

Preparation time: 1 hour 20 minutes | **Cooking time: 10–15 minutes** | **Makes: 12**

Ingredients:
110 g / 4 oz / ⅔ cup self-raising flour, sifted
110 g / 4 oz / ½ cup caster (superfine) sugar
110 g / 4 oz / ½ cup butter, softened
2 large eggs
1 tsp vanilla extract
75 g / 2 ½ oz / ½ cup white chocolate chips

To decorate:
200 g / 7 oz / 1 ⅓ cups white chocolate
200 ml / 7 fl. oz / ¾ cup double (heavy) cream
12 ruby sweets

White chocolate ruby cupcakes

Method

STEP 1
Preheat the oven to 190°C (170°C fan) / 375F / gas 5 and line a 12-hole cupcake tin with paper cases.

STEP 2
Combine the flour, sugar, butter, eggs and vanilla extract in a bowl and whisk together for 2 minutes or until smooth. Fold in the chocolate chips, then divide the mixture between the paper cases.

STEP 3
Transfer the tin to the oven and bake for 10–15 minutes. Test with a wooden toothpick, if it comes out clean, the cakes are done. Transfer the cakes to a wire rack and leave to cool completely.

STEP 4
Finely chop the chocolate and transfer it to a mixing bowl. Heat the cream until it starts to simmer, then pour it over the chocolate and leave to stand for 30 seconds. Slowly stir the chocolate and cream together until it forms a smooth ganache.

STEP 5
Leave the ganache to cool until it's thick enough to hold its shape, then spread it over the cakes and decorate each one with a ruby sweet.

Preparation time: **30 minutes** | Cooking time: **10–15 minutes** | Makes: **12**

Ingredients:

110 g / 4 oz / ⅔ cup self-raising flour, sifted
110 g / 4 oz / ½ cup caster (superfine) sugar
110 g / 4 oz / ½ cup butter, softened
2 large eggs
75 g / 2 ½ oz / ½ cup butterscotch pieces

To decorate:

200 g / 7 oz / ⅔ cup dulce de leche
75 g / 2 ½ oz / ½ cup butterscotch pieces

Butterscotch crunch cupcakes

Method

STEP 1
Preheat the oven to 190°C (170°C fan) / 375F / gas 5 and line a 12-hole cupcake tin with paper cases.

STEP 2
Combine the flour, sugar, butter, eggs and butterscotch pieces in a bowl and whisk together for 2 minutes or until smooth.

STEP 3
Divide the mixture between the cases, then transfer the tin to the oven and bake for 10–15 minutes. Test with a wooden toothpick, if it comes out clean, the cakes are done. Transfer the cakes to a wire rack and leave to cool completely.

STEP 4
Spoon the dulce de leche on top of the cakes and sprinkle with butterscotch pieces.

Preparation time: 40 minutes | Cooking time: 10–15 minutes | Makes: 12

Ingredients:
110 g / 4 oz / ⅔ cup self-raising flour, sifted
110 g / 4 oz / ½ cup caster (superfine) sugar
110 g / 4 oz / ½ cup butter, softened
2 large eggs
1 lime, zest finely grated

To decorate:
110 g / 4 oz / ½ cup butter, softened
225 g / 8 oz / 2 ¼ cups icing (confectioners') sugar, plus extra for dusting
1 tbsp lime juice
a few drops of green food colouring
6 lime slices, halved

Lime buttercream cupcakes

Method

STEP 1
Preheat the oven to 190°C (170°C fan) / 375F / gas 5 and line a 12-hole cupcake tin with paper cases.

STEP 2
Combine the flour, sugar, butter, eggs and lime zest in a bowl and whisk together for 2 minutes or until smooth.

STEP 3
Divide the mixture between the cake cases then transfer the tin to the oven and bake for 10–15 minutes. Test with a wooden toothpick, if it comes out clean, the cakes are done. Transfer the cakes to a wire rack and leave to cool completely.

STEP 4
To make the buttercream, beat the butter until smooth then beat in the icing sugar. Use a whisk to incorporate the lime juice, then whisk for 2 minutes or until well whipped.

STEP 5
Spoon the icing onto the cakes and top each one with half a slice of lime.

Preparation time: **1 hour 10 minutes** | Cooking time: **10–15 minutes** | Makes: **12**

Ingredients:

110 g / 4 oz / ⅔ cup self-raising flour, sifted
110 g / 4 oz / ½ cup caster (superfine) sugar
110 g / 4 oz / ½ cup butter, softened
2 large eggs
1 tsp vanilla extract
75 g / 2 ½ oz / ½ cup white chocolate chips

To decorate:

200 g / 7 oz / 1 ⅓ cups white chocolate
200 ml / 7 fl. oz / ¾ cup double (heavy) cream
12 squares of milk chocolate
cocoa powder for sprinkling

White chocolate ganache cupcakes

Method

STEP 1
Preheat the oven to 190°C (170°C fan) / 375F / gas 5 and line a 12-hole cupcake tin with paper cases.

STEP 2
Combine the flour, sugar, butter, eggs and vanilla extract in a bowl and whisk together for 2 minutes or until smooth. Fold in the chocolate chips, then divide the mixture between the paper cases.

STEP 3
Transfer the tin to the oven and bake for 10–15 minutes. Test with a wooden toothpick, if it comes out clean, the cakes are done. Transfer the cakes to a wire rack and leave to cool completely.

STEP 4
Finely chop the chocolate and transfer it to a mixing bowl. Heat the cream until it starts to simmer, then pour it over the chocolate and leave to stand for 30 seconds. Slowly stir the chocolate and cream together until it forms a smooth ganache.

STEP 5
Leave the ganache to cool until it's thick enough to hold its shape, then spoon it into a piping bag fitted with a large star nozzle. Pipe a swirl on top of each cake and top with the chocolate squares. Finish with a sprinkle of cocoa powder.

Preparation time: **50 minutes** | Cooking time: **15–20 minutes** | Makes: **12**

Ingredients:

175 g / 6 oz / 1 cup light soft brown sugar
2 large eggs
150 ml / 5 fl. oz / ⅔ cup sunflower oil
175 g / 6 oz / 1 ¼ cups plain (all-purpose) flour
2 tsp baking powder
1 tsp ground cinnamon
200 g / 7 oz / 1 ⅔ cups carrots, peeled and coarsely grated

To decorate:

300 ml / 10 ½ fl. oz / 1 ¼ cups double (heavy) cream
2 tbsp icing (confectioners') sugar
100 g / 3 ½ oz / ⅓ cup marzipan
orange food colouring
black food colouring pen

Carrot cupcakes

Method

STEP 1
Preheat the oven to 190°C (170°C fan) / 375F / gas 5 and line a 12-hole cupcake tin with paper cases.

STEP 2
Whisk the sugar, eggs and oil together for 3 minutes. Fold in the flour, baking powder and ground cinnamon, followed by the grated carrots.

STEP 3
Divide the mixture between the paper cases, then transfer the tin to the oven and bake for 15–20 minutes. Test with a wooden toothpick, if it comes out clean, the cakes are done. Transfer the cakes to a wire rack and leave to cool completely.

STEP 4
Whisk the cream with the icing sugar until it holds its shape, then spoon it into a piping bag fitted with a large star nozzle. Pipe a swirl on top of each cake.

STEP 5
Colour the marzipan orange and make it into 12 carrot shapes, drawing on the details with the black food colour pen. Position on top of the cakes.

Preparation time: 1 hour | Cooking time: 10–15 minutes | Makes: 12

Ingredients:

110 g / 4 oz / ⅔ cup self-raising flour, sifted
110 g / 4 oz / ½ cup caster (superfine) sugar
110 g / 4 oz / ½ cup butter, softened
2 large eggs
2 tbsp ground almonds
½ tsp almond extract

To decorate:

200 g / 7 oz / ⅔ cup marzipan
100 g / 3 ½ oz / ⅓ cup ready-to-roll fondant icing
pink food colouring

Battenberg cupcakes

Method

STEP 1
Preheat the oven to 190°C (170°C fan) / 375F / gas 5 and line a 12-hole cupcake tin with paper cases.

STEP 2
Combine the flour, sugar, butter, eggs, ground almonds and almond extract in a bowl and whisk together for 2 minutes or until smooth.

STEP 3
Divide the mixture between the cases, then transfer the tin to the oven and bake for 10–15 minutes. Test with a wooden toothpick, if it comes out clean, the cakes are done. Transfer the cakes to a wire rack and leave to cool completely.

STEP 4
Roll out the marzipan and cut out 12 circles a little smaller in diameter than the surface of the cakes. Wet the backs with a dab of water, then smooth them onto the cakes.

STEP 5
Colour half of the fondant icing pink, then roll out both pieces into a thick rectangle. Cut each piece into 2 strips the same width as they are thick, then stack them so that the colours alternate. Squeeze the strips together, then cut into thick slices and position 1 slice on top of each cake.

STEP 6
Roll any offcuts into tiny balls and dot them around the edges of the cakes.

Preparation time: 45 minutes | **Cooking time: 10–15 minutes** | **Makes: 12**

Ingredients:
110 g / 4 oz / ⅔ cup self-raising flour, sifted
110 g / 4 oz / ½ cup caster (superfine) sugar
110 g / 4 oz / ½ cup butter, softened
2 large eggs
75 g / 2 ½ oz / ½ cup walnuts, chopped
1 tbsp instant espresso powder

To decorate:
100 g / 3 ½ oz / ½ cup butter, softened
200 g / 7 oz / 2 cups icing (confectioners') sugar
2 tsp instant espresso powder
24 walnut halves

Coffee and walnut cupcakes

Method

STEP 1
Preheat the oven to 190°C (170°C fan) / 375F / gas 5 and line a 12-hole cupcake tin with paper cases.

STEP 2
Combine the flour, sugar, butter, eggs, walnuts and espresso powder in a bowl and whisk together for 2 minutes or until smooth.

STEP 3
Divide the mixture between the cases, then transfer the tin to the oven and bake for 10–15 minutes. Test with a wooden toothpick, if it comes out clean, the cakes are done. Transfer the cakes to a wire rack and leave to cool completely.

STEP 4
Beat the butter until smooth, then gradually whisk in the icing sugar and espresso powder.

STEP 5
Spoon the mixture into a piping bag, fitted with a large star nozzle, and pipe a swirl of icing on top of each cake. Top each cake with 2 walnut halves.

Delicious Treats

Preparation time: 50 minutes | **Cooking time: 10–15 minutes** | **Makes: 12**

Ingredients:

110 g / 4 oz / ⅔ cup self-raising flour, sifted
110 g / 4 oz / ½ cup caster (superfine) sugar
110 g / 4 oz / ½ cup butter, softened
2 large eggs
75 g / 2 ½ oz / ½ cup toffee pieces

To decorate:

100 g / 3 ½ oz / ½ cup butter, softened
200 g / 7 oz / 2 cups icing (confectioners') sugar
2 tbsp toffee syrup
12 small squares toffee flapjack

Toffee flapjack cupcakes

Method

STEP 1
Preheat the oven to 190°C (170°C fan) / 375F / gas 5 and line a 12-hole cupcake tin with paper cases.

STEP 2
Combine the flour, sugar, butter, eggs and toffee pieces in a bowl and whisk together for 2 minutes or until smooth.

STEP 3
Divide the mixture between the cases, then transfer the tin to the oven and bake for 10–15 minutes. Test with a wooden toothpick, if it comes out clean, the cakes are done. Transfer the cakes to a wire rack and leave to cool completely.

STEP 4
Beat the butter until smooth, then gradually whisk in the icing sugar and toffee syrup. Spread the buttercream over the cakes and top with the flapjack squares.

Preparation time: **50 minutes** | Cooking time: **10–15 minutes** | Makes: **12**

Ingredients:

110 g / 4 oz / ⅔ cup self-raising flour, sifted
110 g / 4 oz / ½ cup caster (superfine) sugar
110 g / 4 oz / ½ cup butter, softened
2 large eggs
2 tbsp unsweetened cocoa powder

To decorate:

100 g / 3 ½ oz / ½ cup butter, softened
200 g / 7 oz / 2 cups icing (confectioners') sugar
4 chocolate cookies, crushed into crumbs

Cookie crumble cupcakes

Method

STEP 1
Preheat the oven to 190°C (170°C fan) / 375F / gas 5 and line a 12-hole cupcake tin with paper cases.

STEP 2
Combine the flour, sugar, butter, eggs and cocoa in a bowl and whisk together for 2 minutes or until smooth.

STEP 3
Divide the mixture between the cases, then transfer the tin to the oven and bake for 10–15 minutes. Test with a wooden toothpick, if it comes out clean, the cakes are done. Transfer the cakes to a wire rack and leave to cool completely.

STEP 4
Beat the butter until smooth, then gradually whisk in the icing sugar, adding a few drops of water if the mixture is too thick.

STEP 5
Fold in half of the cookie crumbs, then spoon the mixture into a piping bag, fitted with a large star nozzle, and pipe a swirl of icing on top of each cake. Sprinkle over the remaining crumbs to finish.

Preparation time: **50 minutes** | Cooking time: **10–15 minutes** | Makes: **12**

Ingredients:

110 g / 4 oz / ⅔ cup self-raising flour, sifted
110 g / 4 oz / ½ cup caster (superfine) sugar
110 g / 4 oz / ½ cup butter, softened
2 large eggs
1 orange, zest finely grated

To decorate:

100 g / 3 ½ oz / ½ cup butter, softened
200 g / 7 oz / 2 cups icing (confectioners') sugar
2 tbsp unsweetened cocoa powder
1 orange, juiced and zest finely grated
12 mini orange cakes

Mini orange cake cupcakes

Method

STEP 1
Preheat the oven to 190°C (170°C fan) / 375F / gas 5 and line a 12-hole cupcake tin with paper cases.

STEP 2
Combine the flour, sugar, butter, eggs and orange zest in a bowl and whisk together for 2 minutes or until smooth.

STEP 3
Divide the mixture between the cases, then transfer the tin to the oven and bake for 10–15 minutes. Test with a wooden toothpick, if it comes out clean, the cakes are done. Transfer the cakes to a wire rack and leave to cool completely.

STEP 4
Beat the butter until smooth, then gradually whisk in the icing sugar, cocoa, orange zest and 1 tbsp of the orange juice.

STEP 5
Spoon the mixture into a piping bag, fitted with a large star nozzle, and pipe a swirl of icing on top of each cake. Top each cake with a mini orange cake.

Preparation time: 50 minutes | **Cooking time: 10–15 minutes** | **Makes: 12**

Ingredients:

110 g / 4 oz / ⅔ cup self-raising flour, sifted
110 g / 4 oz / ½ cup caster (superfine) sugar
110 g / 4 oz / ½ cup butter, softened
2 large eggs
2 tbsp unsweetened cocoa powder
1 orange, zest finely grated

To decorate:

100 g / 3 ½ oz / ½ cup butter, softened
200 g / 7 oz / 2 cups icing (confectioners') sugar
1 orange, juiced and zest finely grated
12 chocolate orange segments
white chocolate for grating
icing (confectioners') sugar and cocoa powder for dusting

Chocolate orange cupcakes

Method

STEP 1
Preheat the oven to 190°C (170°C fan) / 375F / gas 5 and line a 12-hole cupcake tin with paper cases.

STEP 2
Combine the flour, sugar, butter, eggs, cocoa and orange zest in a bowl and whisk together for 2 minutes or until smooth.

STEP 3
Divide the mixture between the cases, then transfer the tin to the oven and bake for 10–15 minutes. Test with a wooden toothpick, if it comes out clean, the cakes are done. Transfer the cakes to a wire rack and leave to cool completely.

STEP 4
Beat the butter until smooth, then gradually whisk in the icing sugar, orange zest and 1 tbsp of the orange juice.

STEP 5
Spoon the mixture into a piping bag, fitted with a large star nozzle, and pipe a swirl of icing on top of each cake. Insert a chocolate orange segment into each one, then grate over a little white chocolate. Dust lightly with cocoa powder and icing sugar to finish.

Preparation time: 1 hour | **Cooking time: 10–15 minutes** | **Makes: 12**

Ingredients:

110 g / 4 oz / ⅔ cup self-raising flour, sifted
2 tbsp unsweetened cocoa powder
110 g / 4 oz / ½ cup caster (superfine) sugar
110 g / 4 oz / ½ cup butter, softened
2 large eggs
75 g / 2 ½ oz / ½ cup milk chocolate chips

To decorate:

200 g / 7 oz / 1 ¼ cups dark chocolate, minimum 60% cocoa solids
200 ml / 7 fl. oz / ¾ cup double (heavy) cream
chocolate balls, hearts and stars to decorate
edible glitter for sprinkling

Really chocolatey cupcakes

Method

STEP 1
Preheat the oven to 190°C (170°C fan) / 375F / gas 5 and line a 12-hole cupcake tin with paper cases.

STEP 2
Combine the flour, cocoa, sugar, butter and eggs in a bowl and whisk together for 2 minutes or until smooth. Fold in the chocolate chips, then divide the mixture between the paper cases.

STEP 3
Transfer the tin to the oven and bake for 10–15 minutes. Test with a wooden toothpick, if it comes out clean, the cakes are done. Transfer the cakes to a wire rack and leave to cool completely.

STEP 4
Finely chop the chocolate and transfer it to a mixing bowl. Heat the cream until it starts to simmer, then pour it over the chocolate and leave to stand for 30 seconds. Slowly stir the chocolate and cream together until it forms a smooth ganache.

STEP 5
Leave the ganache to cool until it's thick enough to hold its shape, then spoon it into a piping bag fitted with a large star nozzle.

STEP 6
Pipe a swirl of ganache onto each cake and decorate with the chocolate shapes. Finish with a sprinkle of edible glitter.

Preparation time: 45 minutes | **Cooking time:** 10–15 minutes | **Makes:** 12

Ingredients:

110 g / 4 oz / ⅔ cup self-raising flour, sifted
110 g / 4 oz / ½ cup caster (superfine) sugar
110 g / 4 oz / ½ cup butter, softened
2 large eggs
2 tbsp unsweetened cocoa powder

To decorate:

100 g / 3 ½ oz / ½ cup butter, softened
200 g / 7 oz / 2 cups icing (confectioners') sugar
1 tsp vanilla extract
12 chocolate truffles

Chocolate truffle cupcakes

Method

STEP 1
Preheat the oven to 190°C (170°C fan) / 375F / gas 5 and line a 12-hole cupcake tin with paper cases.

STEP 2
Combine the flour, sugar, butter, eggs and cocoa in a bowl and whisk together for 2 minutes or until smooth.

STEP 3
Divide the mixture between the cases, then transfer the tin to the oven and bake for 10–15 minutes. Test with a wooden toothpick, if it comes out clean, the cakes are done. Transfer the cakes to a wire rack and leave to cool completely.

STEP 4
Beat the butter until smooth, then gradually whisk in the icing sugar and vanilla extract.

STEP 5
Spoon the buttercream into a piping bag fitted with a large star nozzle and pipe a swirl on top of each cake. Top with the truffles.

Preparation time: **45 minutes** | Cooking time: **10–15 minutes** | Makes: **12**

Ingredients:

110 g / 4 oz / ⅔ cup self-raising flour, sifted
110 g / 4 oz / ½ cup caster (superfine) sugar
110 g / 4 oz / ½ cup butter, softened
2 large eggs
75 g / 2 ½ oz / ½ cup white chocolate buttons

To decorate:

110 g / 4 oz / ½ cup butter, softened
225 g / 8 oz / 2 ¼ cups icing (confectioners') sugar
2 tbsp unsweetened cocoa powder
2 tbsp milk
100 g / 3 ½ oz / ⅔ cup white chocolate buttons
4 tbsp dark chocolate, melted

White chocolate button cupcakes

Method

STEP 1
Preheat the oven to 190°C (170°C fan) / 375F / gas 5 and line a 12-hole cupcake tin with paper cases.

STEP 2
Combine the flour, sugar, butter, eggs and chocolate buttons in a bowl and whisk together for 2 minutes or until smooth. Divide the mixture between the cases, then transfer the tin to the oven and bake for 10–15 minutes.

STEP 3
Test with a wooden toothpick, if it comes out clean, the cakes are done. Transfer the cakes to a wire rack and leave to cool completely.

STEP 4
To make the buttercream, beat the butter until smooth then beat in the icing sugar, cocoa powder and milk. Spread the buttercream over the cakes and top with the white chocolate buttons before drizzling with dark chocolate.

Preparation time: **45 minutes** | Cooking time: **10–15 minutes** | Makes: **12**

Ingredients:

110 g / 4 oz / ⅔ cup self-raising flour, sifted
110 g / 4 oz / ½ cup caster (superfine) sugar
110 g / 4 oz / ½ cup butter, softened
2 large eggs
1 tsp vanilla extract
2 tbsp unsweetened cocoa powder

To decorate:

110 g / 4 oz / ½ cup butter, softened
225 g / 8 oz / 2 ¼ cups icing (confectioners') sugar
2 tbsp unsweetened cocoa powder
2 tbsp milk

Chocolate butterfly cakes

Method

STEP 1
Preheat the oven to 190°C (170°C fan) / 375F / gas 5 and line a 12-hole cupcake tin with paper cases.

STEP 2
Combine the flour, sugar, butter, eggs, vanilla extract and cocoa in a bowl and whisk together for 2 minutes or until smooth.

STEP 3
Divide the mixture between the cake cases then transfer the tin to the oven and bake for 10–15 minutes. Test with a wooden toothpick, if it comes out clean, the cakes are done. Transfer the cakes to a wire rack and leave to cool completely.

STEP 4
To make the buttercream, beat the butter until smooth then beat in the icing sugar and cocoa. Use a whisk to incorporate the milk, then whisk for 2 minutes or until well whipped.

STEP 5
Spoon the icing into a piping bag fitted with a large star nozzle. Using a sharp knife, cut a shallow cone out of the centre of each cake and reserve.

STEP 6
Pipe a swirl of buttercream into the centre of each cake. Take the reserved cake pieces and cut each one in half then arrange on the buttercream to make the butterfly wings.

Preparation time: **1 hour 20 minutes** | Cooking time: **10–15 minutes** | Makes: **12**

Ingredients:

110 g / 4 oz / ⅔ cup self-raising flour, sifted
2 tbsp unsweetened cocoa powder
110 g / 4 oz / ½ cup caster (superfine) sugar
110 g / 4 oz / ½ cup butter, softened
2 large eggs
1 tsp vanilla extract
75 g / 2 ½ oz / ½ cup white chocolate chips

To decorate:

200 g / 7 oz / 1 ⅓ cup white chocolate
200 ml / 7 fl. oz / ¾ cup double (heavy) cream
50 g / 1 ¾ oz / 1 cup striped chocolate curls

Double chocolate curl cupcakes

Method

STEP 1
Preheat the oven to 190°C (170°C fan) / 375F / gas 5 and line a 12-hole cupcake tin with paper cases.

STEP 2
Combine the flour, cocoa, sugar, butter, eggs and vanilla extract in a bowl and whisk together for 2 minutes or until smooth. Fold in the chocolate chips, then divide the mixture between the paper cases.

STEP 3
Transfer the tin to the oven and bake for 10–15 minutes. Test with a wooden toothpick, if it comes out clean, the cakes are done. Transfer the cakes to a wire rack and leave to cool completely.

STEP 4
Finely chop the chocolate and transfer it to a mixing bowl. Heat the cream until it starts to simmer, then pour it over the chocolate and leave to stand for 30 seconds. Slowly stir the chocolate and cream together until it forms a smooth ganache.

STEP 5
Leave the ganache to cool until it's thick enough to hold its shape, then spread it over the cakes and sprinkle with chocolate curls.

Preparation time: 50 minutes | Cooking time: 10–15 minutes | Makes: 12

Ingredients:

110 g / 4 oz / ⅔ cup self-raising flour, sifted
110 g / 4 oz / ½ cup caster (superfine) sugar
110 g / 4 oz / ½ cup butter, softened
2 large eggs
75 g / 2 ½ oz / ½ cup white chocolate chips

To decorate:

100 g / 3 ½ oz / ½ cup butter, softened
200 g / 7 oz / 2 cups icing (confectioners') sugar
50 g / 1 ¾ oz / ⅓ cup white chocolate, melted
6 chocolate flakes, halved
icing (confectioners') sugar to dust

White chocolate cupcakes

Method

STEP 1
Preheat the oven to 190°C (170°C fan) / 375F / gas 5 and line a 12-hole cupcake tin with paper cases.

STEP 2
Combine the flour, sugar, butter, eggs and chocolate chips in a bowl and whisk together for 2 minutes or until smooth.

STEP 3
Divide the mixture between the cases, then transfer the tin to the oven and bake for 10–15 minutes. Test with a wooden toothpick, if it comes out clean, the cakes are done. Transfer the cakes to a wire rack and leave to cool completely.

STEP 4
Beat the butter until smooth, then gradually whisk in the icing sugar and melted white chocolate.

STEP 5
Spoon the mixture into a piping bag, fitted with a large star nozzle, and pipe a swirl of icing on top of each cake. Insert half a chocolate flake into each one and finish with a dusting of icing sugar.

Preparation time: **45 minutes** | **Cooking time:** **10–15 minutes** | **Makes:** **12**

Ingredients:

110 g / 4 oz / ⅔ cup self-raising flour, sifted
110 g / 4 oz / ½ cup caster (superfine) sugar
110 g / 4 oz / ½ cup butter, softened
2 large eggs
2 tbsp unsweetened cocoa powder
1 tbsp malted milk powder

To decorate:

100 g / 3 ½ oz / ½ cup butter, softened
200 g / 7 oz / 2 cups icing (confectioners') sugar
2 tbsp cocoa powder
2 tsp instant malted milk powder
12 chocolate balls
milk chocolate for grating

Chocolate ball cupcakes

Method

STEP 1
Preheat the oven to 190°C (170°C fan) / 375F / gas 5 and line a 12-hole cupcake tin with paper cases.

STEP 2
Combine the flour, sugar, butter, eggs, cocoa and malted milk powder in a bowl and whisk together for 2 minutes or until smooth.

STEP 3
Divide the mixture between the cases, then transfer the tin to the oven and bake for 10–15 minutes. Test with a wooden toothpick, if it comes out clean, the cakes are done. Transfer the cakes to a wire rack and leave to cool completely.

STEP 4
Beat the butter until smooth, then gradually whisk in the icing sugar, cocoa and malted milk powder.

STEP 5
Spoon the mixture into a piping bag, fitted with a large star nozzle, and pipe a swirl of icing on top of each cake. Top each cake with a chocolate ball and grate over a little milk chocolate to finish.

Preparation time: **45 minutes** | Cooking time: **10–15 minutes** | Makes: **12**

Ingredients:

110 g / 4 oz / ⅔ cup self-raising flour, sifted
110 g / 4 oz / ½ cup caster (superfine) sugar
110 g / 4 oz / ½ cup butter, softened
2 large eggs
2 tbsp unsweetened cocoa powder
1 tbsp instant espresso powder

To decorate:

100 g / 3 ½ oz / ½ cup butter, softened
200 g / 7 oz / 2 cups icing (confectioners') sugar
2 tbsp cocoa powder
2 tsp instant espresso powder
36 chocolate coated coffee beans

Mocha cupcakes

Method

STEP 1
Preheat the oven to 190°C (170°C fan) / 375F / gas 5 and line a 12-hole cupcake tin with paper cases.

STEP 2
Combine the flour, sugar, butter, eggs, cocoa and espresso powder in a bowl and whisk together for 2 minutes or until smooth.

STEP 3
Divide the mixture between the cases, then transfer the tin to the oven and bake for 10–15 minutes. Test with a wooden toothpick, if it comes out clean, the cakes are done. Transfer the cakes to a wire rack and leave to cool completely.

STEP 4
Beat the butter until smooth, then gradually whisk in the icing sugar, cocoa and espresso powder.

STEP 5
Spoon the mixture into a piping bag, fitted with a large star nozzle, and pipe a swirl of icing on top of each cake. Top each cake with 3 chocolate coated coffee beans.

Preparation time: 1 hour | **Cooking time: 10–15 minutes** | **Makes: 12**

Ingredients:

110 g / 4 oz / ⅔ cup self-raising flour, sifted
2 tbsp unsweetened cocoa powder
110 g / 4 oz / ½ cup caster (superfine) sugar
110 g / 4 oz / ½ cup butter, softened
2 large eggs
75 g / 2 ½ oz / ½ cup white chocolate chips
75 g / 2 ½ oz / ½ cup milk chocolate chips

To decorate:

200 g / 7 oz / 1 cup dark chocolate, minimum 60% cocoa solids
200 ml / 7 fl. oz / ¾ cup double (heavy) cream
milk, white and dark chocolate balls to decorate

Triple chocolate cupcakes

Method

STEP 1
Preheat the oven to 190°C (170°C fan) / 375F / gas 5 and line a 12-hole cupcake tin with paper cases.

STEP 2
Combine the flour, cocoa, sugar, butter and eggs in a bowl and whisk together for 2 minutes or until smooth. Fold in the chocolate chips, then divide the mixture between the paper cases.

STEP 3
Transfer the tin to the oven and bake for 10–15 minutes. Test with a wooden toothpick, if it comes out clean, the cakes are done. Transfer the cakes to a wire rack and leave to cool completely.

STEP 4
Finely chop the chocolate and transfer it to a mixing bowl. Heat the cream until it starts to simmer, then pour it over the chocolate and leave to stand for 30 seconds. Slowly stir the chocolate and cream together until it forms a smooth ganache.

STEP 5
Leave the ganache to cool until it's thick enough to hold its shape, then spoon it into a piping bag fitted with a large star nozzle.

STEP 6
Pipe a swirl of ganache onto each cake and sprinkle with chocolate balls.

Preparation time: 45 minutes | Cooking time: 10–15 minutes | Makes: 12

Ingredients:

110 g / 4 oz / ⅔ cup self-raising flour, sifted
110 g / 4 oz / ½ cup caster (superfine) sugar
110 g / 4 oz / ½ cup butter, softened
1 tsp vanilla extract
2 large eggs

To decorate:

400 ml / 14 fl. oz / 1 ⅔ cups double (heavy) cream
6 tbsp blackberry jam (jelly)
icing (confectioners') sugar for dusting

Blackberry cream cupcakes

Method

STEP 1
Preheat the oven to 190°C (170°C fan) / 375F / gas 5 and line a 12-hole cupcake tin with paper cases.

STEP 2
Measure the cake ingredients into a bowl then whisk together for 3 minutes or until smooth and light. Divide the mixture between the paper cases, then transfer the tin to the oven and bake for 10–15 minutes.

STEP 3
Test the cakes with a toothpick; if it comes out clean, the cakes are done. Transfer the cakes to a wire rack and leave to cool completely.

STEP 4
Whip the cream until it holds its shape, then spoon it into a piping bag fitted with a large star nozzle and pipe a ring of rosettes around the edge of each cake.

STEP 5
Fill the centres with blackberry jam, then dust them lightly with icing sugar.

Preparation time: 1 hour | **Cooking time: 10–15 minutes** | **Makes: 12**

Ingredients:
110 g / 4 oz / ⅔ cup self-raising flour, sifted
2 tbsp unsweetened cocoa powder
110 g / 4 oz / ½ cup caster (superfine) sugar
110 g / 4 oz / ½ cup butter, softened
2 large eggs
75 g / 2 ½ oz / ⅓ cup glacé cherries, chopped

To decorate:
4 tbsp black cherry jam (jelly)
200 ml / 7 fl. oz / ¾ cup double (heavy) cream
12 pitted black cherries in kirsch, drained
milk chocolate for grating

Black forest cupcakes

Method

STEP 1
Preheat the oven to 190°C (170°C fan) / 375F / gas 5 and line a 12-hole cupcake tin with paper cases.

STEP 2
Combine the flour, cocoa, sugar, butter and eggs in a bowl and whisk together for 2 minutes or until smooth. Fold in the cherries, then divide the mixture between the paper cases.

STEP 3
Transfer the tin to the oven and bake for 10–15 minutes. Test with a wooden toothpick, if it comes out clean, the cakes are done. Transfer the cakes to a wire rack and leave to cool completely.

STEP 4
Spread the top of each cake with cherry jam. Whip the cream until it holds its shape, then spoon it into a piping bag fitted with a large star nozzle. Pipe a ring around the edge of each cake.

STEP 5
Top each cake with a black cherry, then grate over a little milk chocolate.

Preparation time: 40 minutes | **Cooking time: 10–15 minutes** | **Makes: 12**

Ingredients:

110 g / 4 oz / ⅔ cup self-raising flour, sifted
2 tbsp unsweetened cocoa powder
110 g / 4 oz / ½ cup caster (superfine) sugar
110 g / 4 oz / ½ cup butter, softened
2 large eggs
75 g / 2 ½ oz / ½ cup roasted hazelnuts (cobnuts), chopped

To decorate:

400 ml / 14 fl. oz / 1 ½ cups hazelnut chocolate spread

Hazelnut chocolate cupcakes

Method

STEP 1
Preheat the oven to 190°C (170°C fan) / 375F / gas 5 and line a 12-hole cupcake tin with paper cases.

STEP 2
Combine the flour, cocoa, sugar, butter and eggs in a bowl and whisk together for 2 minutes or until smooth. Fold in the hazelnuts, then divide the mixture between the paper cases.

STEP 3
Transfer the tin to the oven and bake for 10–15 minutes. Test with a wooden toothpick, if it comes out clean, the cakes are done. Transfer the cakes to a wire rack and leave to cool completely.

STEP 4
Spoon the chocolate spread into a piping bag fitted with a large plain nozzle, then pipe a big swirl on top of each cake.

Preparation time: 45 minutes | **Cooking time:** 10–15 minutes | **Makes:** 12

Ingredients:

110 g / 4 oz / ⅔ cup self-raising flour, sifted
110 g / 4 oz / ½ cup caster (superfine) sugar
110 g / 4 oz / ½ cup butter, softened
2 large eggs
2 tbsp unsweetened cocoa powder

To decorate:

100 g / 3 ½ oz / ½ cup butter, softened
200 g / 7 oz / 2 cups icing (confectioners') sugar
2 tbsp cocoa powder
12 white chocolate cigarillos
chocolate vermicelli for sprinkling

Chocolate buttercream cupcakes

Method

STEP 1
Preheat the oven to 190°C (170°C fan) / 375F / gas 5 and line a 12-hole cupcake tin with paper cases.

STEP 2
Combine the flour, sugar, butter, eggs and cocoa in a bowl and whisk together for 2 minutes or until smooth.

STEP 3
Divide the mixture between the cases, then transfer the tin to the oven and bake for 10–15 minutes. Test with a wooden toothpick, if it comes out clean, the cakes are done. Transfer the cakes to a wire rack and leave to cool completely.

STEP 4
Beat the butter until smooth, then gradually whisk in the icing sugar and cocoa powder.

STEP 5
Spoon the buttercream onto the cakes and insert a white chocolate cigarillo into each one. Finish with a sprinkle of chocolate vermicelli.

Preparation time: 1 hour 10 minutes | **Cooking time: 10–15 minutes** | **Makes: 12**

Ingredients:

110 g / 4 oz / ⅔ cup self-raising flour, sifted
110 g / 4 oz / ½ cup caster (superfine) sugar
110 g / 4 oz / ½ cup butter, softened
2 large eggs
1 tsp vanilla extract
75 g / 2 ½ oz / ½ cup white chocolate chips
2 tbsp freeze-dried raspberry pieces

To decorate:

200 g / 7 oz / 1 ⅓ cups white chocolate
200 ml / 7 fl. oz / ⅔ cup double (heavy) cream
12 raspberries
white chocolate for grating

White chocolate and raspberry cupcakes

Method

STEP 1
Preheat the oven to 190°C (170°C fan) / 375F / gas 5 and line a 12-hole cupcake tin with paper cases.

STEP 2
Combine the flour, sugar, butter, eggs and vanilla extract in a bowl and whisk together for 2 minutes or until smooth. Fold in the chocolate chips and raspberry pieces, then divide the mixture between the paper cases.

STEP 3
Transfer the tin to the oven and bake for 10–15 minutes. Test with a wooden toothpick, if it comes out clean, the cakes are done. Transfer the cakes to a wire rack and leave to cool completely.

STEP 4
Finely chop the chocolate and transfer it to a mixing bowl. Heat the cream until it starts to simmer, then pour it over the chocolate and leave to stand for 30 seconds. Slowly stir the chocolate and cream together until it forms a smooth ganache.

STEP 5
Leave the ganache to cool until it's thick enough to hold its shape, then spoon it into a piping bag fitted with a large star nozzle. Pipe a swirl on top of each cake and top with the raspberries. Grate over a little white chocolate to finish.

Preparation time: **1 hour** | Cooking time: **10–15 minutes** | Makes: **12**

Ingredients:

110 g / 4 oz / ⅔ cup self-raising flour, sifted
2 tbsp unsweetened cocoa powder
110 g / 4 oz / ½ cup caster (superfine) sugar
110 g / 4 oz / ½ cup butter, softened
2 large eggs
75 g / 2 ½ oz / ½ cup dark chocolate chips

To decorate:

200 g / 7 oz / 1 ⅓ cups dark chocolate, minimum 60% cocoa solids
200 ml / 7 fl. oz / ¾ cup double (heavy) cream
dark chocolate chips to decorate

Dark chocolate ganache cupcakes

Method

STEP 1
Preheat the oven to 190°C (170°C fan) / 375F / gas 5 and line a 12-hole cupcake tin with paper cases.

STEP 2
Combine the flour, cocoa, sugar, butter and eggs in a bowl and whisk together for 2 minutes or until smooth. Fold in the chocolate chips, then divide the mixture between the paper cases.

STEP 3
Transfer the tin to the oven and bake for 10–15 minutes. Test with a wooden toothpick, if it comes out clean, the cakes are done. Transfer the cakes to a wire rack and leave to cool completely.

STEP 4
Finely chop the chocolate and transfer it to a mixing bowl. Heat the cream until it starts to simmer, then pour it over the chocolate and leave to stand for 30 seconds. Slowly stir the chocolate and cream together until it forms a smooth ganache.

STEP 5
Leave the ganache to cool until it's thick enough to hold its shape, then spread it onto the cakes. Decorate with the chocolate chips.

Preparation time: **1 hour** | **Cooking time:** **10–15 minutes** | **Makes:** **12**

Ingredients:

110 g / 4 oz / ⅔ cup self-raising flour, sifted
2 tbsp unsweetened cocoa powder
110 g / 4 oz / ½ cup caster (superfine) sugar
110 g / 4 oz / ½ cup butter, softened
2 large eggs
75 g / 2 ½ oz / ½ cup milk chocolate chips

To decorate:

200 g / 7 oz / 1 ⅓ cups dark chocolate, minimum 60% cocoa solids
200 g / 7 oz / 1 ⅓ cups white chocolate
400 ml / 14 fl. oz / 1 ⅔ cups double (heavy) cream
white chocolate cigarillos to decorate

Double chocolate ganache cupcakes

Method

STEP 1
Preheat the oven to 190°C (170°C fan) / 375F / gas 5 and line a 12-hole cupcake tin with paper cases.

STEP 2
Combine the flour, cocoa, sugar, butter and eggs in a bowl and whisk together for 2 minutes or until smooth. Fold in the chocolate chips, then divide the mixture between the paper cases.

STEP 3
Transfer the tin to the oven and bake for 10–15 minutes. Test with a wooden toothpick, if it comes out clean, the cakes are done. Transfer the cakes to a wire rack and leave to cool completely.

STEP 4
Finely chop both types of chocolate and transfer them to separate mixing bowls. Heat the cream until it starts to simmer, then pour half into each bowl and leave to stand for 30 seconds. Slowly stir the chocolate and cream together until it forms a smooth ganache.

STEP 5
Leave the ganache mixtures to cool until they're thick enough to hold their shape, then spoon them into 2 piping bags fitted with large star nozzles.

STEP 6
Pipe the white chocolate ganache on first and top with a swirl of dark chocolate ganache. Decorate with the cigarillos.

Children's & Novelty

Preparation time: **1 hour 30 minutes** | Cooking time: **10–15 minutes** | Makes: **12**

Ingredients:

110 g / 4 oz / ⅔ cup self-raising flour, sifted
110 g / 4 oz / ½ cup caster (superfine) sugar
110 g / 4 oz / ½ cup butter, softened
2 large eggs
2 tbsp unsweetened cocoa powder

To decorate:

100 g / 3 ½ oz / ½ cup butter, softened
200 g / 7 oz / 2 cups icing (confectioners') sugar
2 tbsp cocoa powder
1 tbsp milk
12 peppermint chocolate sticks, broken into pieces
400 g / 14 oz / 1 ½ cups ready-to-roll fondant icing
blue, purple, yellow and green food colouring
black food colouring pen

Dickybird cupcakes

Method

STEP 1
Preheat the oven to 190°C (170°C fan) / 375F / gas 5 and line a 12-hole cupcake tin with paper cases.

STEP 2
Combine the flour, sugar, butter, eggs and cocoa powder in a bowl and whisk together for 2 minutes or until smooth.

STEP 3
Divide the mixture between the cases, then transfer the tin to the oven and bake for 10–15 minutes. Test with a wooden toothpick, if it comes out clean, the cakes are done. Transfer the cakes to a wire rack and leave to cool completely.

STEP 4
Beat the butter until smooth, then gradually whisk in the icing sugar, cocoa powder and milk. Spoon the mixture into a piping bag, fitted with a large star nozzle, and pipe a swirl of icing on top of each cake. Arrange the chocolate stick pieces into a nest shape on top of the cakes.

STEP 5
Divide the fondant icing into 4 pieces. Colour 3 pieces blue, purple and yellow and use each colour to model 4 pairs of birds. Use some of the yellow off-cuts for the beaks, then use some of the remaining white icing to make the eyes, adding the pupils with the black food colour pen.

STEP 6
Colour the rest of the icing green and shape it into leaves to decorate the nests.

Preparation time: **1 hour 30 minutes** | Cooking time: **10–15 minutes** | Makes: **12**

Ingredients:

110 g / 4 oz / ⅔ cup self-raising flour, sifted
110 g / 4 oz / ½ cup caster (superfine) sugar
110 g / 4 oz / ½ cup butter, softened
2 large eggs
1 tsp vanilla extract

To decorate:

150 g / 5 ½ oz / 1 ½ cups icing (confectioners') sugar
200 g / 7 oz / ¾ cup ready-to-roll fondant icing
black, green, blue and yellow food colouring

Racing car cupcakes

Method

STEP 1
Preheat the oven to 190°C (170°C fan) / 375F / gas 5 and line a 12-hole cupcake tin with paper cases.

STEP 2
Combine the flour, sugar, butter, eggs and vanilla extract in a bowl and whisk together for 2 minutes or until smooth. Divide the mixture between the cases, then transfer the tin to the oven and bake for 10–15 minutes.

STEP 3
Test with a wooden toothpick, if it comes out clean, the cakes are done. Transfer the cakes to a wire rack and leave to cool completely.

STEP 4
Add a little water to the icing sugar, a few drops at a time, until it forms a smooth, spreadable icing. Reserve a little icing for the decoration, then spoon the rest onto the cakes and tap them lightly on the work surface to level it out into a smooth puddle.

STEP 5
Colour a quarter of the fondant icing grey, then roll it out and cut out 12 circles. Lay the circles on top of the cakes and add a little more black food colouring to the off-cuts before shaping them into the wheels and helmet visors.

STEP 6
Make 12 helmets from a small piece of the white fondant, then divide the rest into 3 pieces and colour them green, blue and yellow. Model them into the cars, then assemble everything on top of the cakes.

Preparation time: **1 hour 30 minutes** | Cooking time: **10–15 minutes** | Makes: **12**

Ingredients:

110 g / 4 oz / ⅔ cup self-raising flour, sifted
110 g / 4 oz / ½ cup caster (superfine) sugar
110 g / 4 oz / ½ cup butter, softened
2 large eggs
1 tsp vanilla extract

To decorate:

150 g / 5 ½ oz / 1 ½ cups icing (confectioners') sugar
200 g / 7 oz / ¾ cup ready-to-roll fondant icing
blue, purple, pink and yellow food colouring
black food colour pen

Flutterby cupcakes

Method

STEP 1
Preheat the oven to 190°C (170°C fan) / 375F / gas 5 and line a 12-hole cupcake tin with paper cases.

STEP 2
Combine the flour, sugar, butter, eggs and vanilla extract in a bowl and whisk together for 2 minutes or until smooth. Divide the mixture between the cases, then transfer the tin to the oven and bake for 10–15 minutes.

STEP 3
Test with a wooden toothpick, if it comes out clean, the cakes are done. Transfer the cakes to a wire rack and leave to cool completely.

STEP 4
Add a little water to the icing sugar, a few drops at a time, until it forms a smooth, spreadable icing. Spoon the icing onto the cakes and tap them lightly on the work surface to level it out into a smooth puddle.

STEP 5
Colour a quarter of the fondant icing yellow, then roll it out and cut out 12 large flowers. Lay them on top of the cakes. Save a small piece of white fondant, then split the rest into 3 pieces and colour them blue, purple and pink. Model some of the coloured fondant into the butterfly bodies, then roll out the rest and use a heart-shaped cutter to make the wings.

STEP 6
Cut out the flowers with blossom-shaped plunger cutters and apply them directly onto the cakes. Use the reserved white icing for the details and eyes, adding the pupils with a black food colour pen.

Preparation time: 40 minutes | Cooking time: 10–15 minutes | Makes: 12

Ingredients:
110 g / 4 oz / ⅔ cup self-raising flour, sifted
110 g / 4 oz / ½ cup caster (superfine) sugar
110 g / 4 oz / ½ cup butter, softened
2 large eggs
1 tsp vanilla extract

To decorate:
110 g / 4 oz / ½ cup butter, softened
225 g / 8 oz / 2 ¼ cups icing (confectioners') sugar, plus extra for dusting
2 tbsp milk
1 tsp vanilla extract
hundreds and thousands for sprinkling
12 colourful sweets
12 lollipops

Lollipop cupcakes

Method

STEP 1
Preheat the oven to 190°C (170°C fan) / 375F / gas 5 and line a 12-hole cupcake tin with paper cases.

STEP 2
Combine the flour, sugar, butter, eggs and vanilla extract in a bowl and whisk together for 2 minutes or until smooth.

STEP 3
Divide the mixture between the cake cases then transfer the tin to the oven and bake for 10–15 minutes. Test with a wooden toothpick, if it comes out clean, the cakes are done. Transfer the cakes to a wire rack and leave to cool completely.

STEP 4
To make the buttercream, beat the butter until smooth then beat in the icing sugar. Use a whisk to incorporate the milk and vanilla extract, then whisk for 2 minutes or until well whipped.

STEP 5
Spoon the icing into a piping bag fitted with a large star nozzle. Pipe a big swirl on top of each cake and sprinkle with hundreds and thousands. Top each cake with a sweet and stick a lollipop in the side.

Preparation time: **50 minutes** | Cooking time: **10–15 minutes** | Makes: **12**

Ingredients:

110 g / 4 oz / ⅔ cup self-raising flour, sifted
110 g / 4 oz / ½ cup caster (superfine) sugar
110 g / 4 oz / ½ cup butter, softened
2 large eggs
75 g / 2 ½ oz / ½ cup caramel pieces

To decorate:

100 g / 3 ½ oz / ½ cup butter, softened
200 g / 7 oz / 2 cups icing (confectioners') sugar
2 tbsp caramel syrup
200 g / 7 oz / 2 cups caramel-coated popcorn

Caramel popcorn cupcakes

Method

STEP 1
Preheat the oven to 190°C (170°C fan) / 375F / gas 5 and line a 12-hole cupcake tin with paper cases.

STEP 2
Combine the flour, sugar, butter, eggs and caramel pieces in a bowl and whisk together for 2 minutes or until smooth.

STEP 3
Divide the mixture between the cases, then transfer the tin to the oven and bake for 10–15 minutes. Test with a wooden toothpick, if it comes out clean, the cakes are done. Transfer the cakes to a wire rack and leave to cool completely.

STEP 4
Beat the butter until smooth, then gradually whisk in the icing sugar and caramel syrup. Spread the buttercream over the cakes and top with popcorn.

Preparation time: **50 minutes** | Cooking time: **10–15 minutes** | Makes: **12**

Ingredients:

110 g / 4 oz / ⅔ cup self-raising flour, sifted
110 g / 4 oz / ½ cup caster (superfine) sugar
110 g / 4 oz / ½ cup butter, softened
2 large eggs
2 tbsp unsweetened cocoa powder
a few drops of peppermint essence

To decorate:

100 g / 3 ½ oz / ½ cup butter, softened
200 g / 7 oz / 2 cups icing (confectioners') sugar
a few drops of peppermint essence
100 g / 3 ½ oz / ½ cup ready-to-roll fondant icing

Peppermint candy cane cupcakes

Method

STEP 1
Preheat the oven to 190°C (170°C fan) / 375F / gas 5 and line a 12-hole cupcake tin with paper cases.

STEP 2
Combine the flour, sugar, butter, eggs, cocoa and peppermint essence in a bowl and whisk together for 2 minutes or until smooth.

STEP 3
Divide the mixture between the cases, then transfer the tin to the oven and bake for 10–15 minutes. Test with a wooden toothpick, if it comes out clean, the cakes are done. Transfer the cakes to a wire rack and leave to cool completely.

STEP 4
Beat the butter until smooth, then gradually whisk in the icing sugar and peppermint essence. Spread the buttercream over the cakes.

STEP 5
Roll the fondant icing into a long thin sausage, then cut it into 12 pieces. Curve the tops over to form the candy canes and position on top of the cakes.

Preparation time: **50 minutes** | Cooking time: **10–15 minutes** | Makes: **12**

Ingredients:
110 g / 4 oz / ⅔ cup self-raising flour, sifted
110 g / 4 oz / ½ cup caster (superfine) sugar
110 g / 4 oz / ½ cup butter, softened
2 large eggs
1 tsp vanilla extract
75 g / 2 ½ oz / ½ cup white chocolate chips

To decorate:
200 g / 7 oz white chocolate
200 ml / 7 fl. oz / ¾ cup double (heavy) cream
2 tbsp soft light brown sugar
36 white chocolate seashells

White chocolate seashell cupcakes

Method

STEP 1
Preheat the oven to 190°C (170°C fan) / 375F / gas 5 and line a 12-hole cupcake tin with paper cases.

STEP 2
Combine the flour, sugar, butter, eggs and vanilla extract in a bowl and whisk together for 2 minutes or until smooth. Fold in the chocolate chips, then divide the mixture between the paper cases.

STEP 3
Transfer the tin to the oven and bake for 10–15 minutes. Test with a wooden toothpick, if it comes out clean, the cakes are done. Transfer the cakes to a wire rack and leave to cool completely.

STEP 4
Finely chop the chocolate and transfer it to a mixing bowl. Heat the cream until it starts to simmer, then pour it over the chocolate and leave to stand for 30 seconds. Slowly stir the chocolate and cream together until it forms a smooth ganache.

STEP 5
Leave the ganache to cool until it's thick enough to hold its shape, then spoon it into a piping bag fitted with a large star nozzle. Pipe a swirl onto each cake and add a little brown sugar 'sand' before topping with the seashells.

Preparation time: 1 hour | Cooking time: 10–15 minutes | Makes: 12

Ingredients:
110 g / 4 oz / ⅔ cup self-raising flour, sifted
110 g / 4 oz / ½ cup caster (superfine) sugar
110 g / 4 oz / ½ cup butter, softened
2 large eggs
1 tsp vanilla extract

To decorate:
110 g / 4 oz / ½ cup butter, softened
225 g / 8 oz / 2 ¼ cups icing (confectioners') sugar
2 tbsp milk
1 tsp vanilla extract
75 g / 2 ½ oz / 1 ¼ cups mini marshmallows
100 g / 3 ½ oz / ½ cup ready-to-roll fondant icing
black food colouring
12 sugar flowers

Marshmallow sheep cupcakes

Method

STEP 1
Preheat the oven to 190°C (170°C fan) / 375F / gas 5 and line a 12-hole cupcake tin with paper cases.

STEP 2
Combine the flour, sugar, butter, eggs and vanilla extract in a bowl and whisk together for 2 minutes or until smooth.

STEP 3
Divide the mixture between the cake cases then transfer the tin to the oven and bake for 10–15 minutes. Test with a wooden toothpick, if it comes out clean, the cakes are done. Transfer the cakes to a wire rack and leave to cool completely.

STEP 4
To make the buttercream, beat the butter until smooth then beat in the icing sugar. Use a whisk to incorporate the milk and vanilla extract, then whisk for 2 minutes or until well whipped.

STEP 5
Spread the buttercream onto the cakes and top with the marshmallows.

STEP 6
Reserve a small piece of white fondant icing for the eyes and colour the rest grey. Shape into the sheep heads, ears and pupils, adding the whites of the eyes with the reserved fondant. Position the heads on top of the cakes and add a sugar flower to each one.

Preparation time: **45 minutes** | Cooking time: **10–15 minutes** | Makes: **12**

Ingredients:

110 g / 4 oz / ⅔ cup self-raising flour, sifted
110 g / 4 oz / ½ cup caster (superfine) sugar
110 g / 4 oz / ½ cup butter, softened
2 large eggs
1 tsp vanilla extract

To decorate:

100 g / 3 ½ oz / ½ cup butter, softened
200 g / 7 oz / 2 cups icing (confectioners') sugar
2 tbsp unsweetened cocoa powder
100 g / 3 ½ oz / ½ cup pale blue ready-to-roll fondant icing

Fondant fish cupcakes

Method

STEP 1
Preheat the oven to 190°C (170°C fan) / 375F / gas 5 and line a 12-hole cupcake tin with paper cases.

STEP 2
Combine the flour, sugar, butter, eggs and vanilla extract in a bowl and whisk together for 2 minutes or until smooth.

STEP 3
Divide the mixture between the cases, then transfer the tin to the oven and bake for 10–15 minutes. Test with a wooden toothpick, if it comes out clean, the cakes are done. Transfer the cakes to a wire rack and leave to cool completely.

STEP 4
Beat the butter until smooth, then gradually whisk in the icing sugar and cocoa powder.

STEP 5
Spoon the buttercream into a piping bag fitted with a large star nozzle and pipe it onto the cakes.

STEP 6
Roll out the blue fondant icing and use a fish cutter to cut out 12 fish shapes. Lay them on top of the cakes.

Preparation time: **1 hour 30 minutes** | Cooking time: **10–15 minutes** | Makes: **12**

Ingredients:

110 g / 4 oz / ⅔ cup self-raising flour, sifted
110 g / 4 oz / ½ cup caster (superfine) sugar
110 g / 4 oz / ½ cup butter, softened
2 large eggs
½ tsp rosewater
½ tsp orange flower water

To decorate:

400 g / 14 oz / 1 ½ cups ready-to-roll fondant icing
yellow, orange, purple and green food colouring

Spring flower cupcakes

Method

STEP 1
Preheat the oven to 190°C (170°C fan) / 375F / gas 5 and line a 12-hole cupcake tin with paper cases.

STEP 2
Combine the flour, sugar, butter, eggs and flower waters in a bowl and whisk together for 2 minutes or until smooth. Divide the mixture between the cases, then transfer the tin to the oven and bake for 10–15 minutes.

STEP 3
Test with a wooden toothpick, if it comes out clean, the cakes are done. Transfer the cakes to a wire rack and leave to cool completely.

STEP 4
Roll out half of the fondant icing and cut out 12 circles slightly smaller than the top of the cakes. Wet the backs with a dab of water and smooth them onto the cakes.

STEP 5
Colour the rest of the icing yellow, orange, purple and green and model it into the flowers, leaves and stalks. Attach to the icing with a dab of water as before.

Preparation time: **50 minutes** | Cooking time: **10–15 minutes** | Makes: **12**

Ingredients:

110 g / 4 oz /   cup self-raising flour, sifted
110 g / 4 oz / ½ cup caster (superfine) sugar
110 g / 4 oz / ½ cup butter, softened
2 large eggs
75 g / 2 ½ oz / ½ cup butterscotch pieces

To decorate:

100 g / 3 ½ oz / ½ cup butter, softened
200 g / 7 oz / 2 cups icing (confectioners') sugar
2 tbsp butterscotch syrup
4 tbsp soft light brown sugar
12 seashell sweets

Fossil beach cupcakes

Method

STEP 1
Preheat the oven to 190°C (170°C fan) / 375F / gas 5 and line a 12-hole cupcake tin with paper cases.

STEP 2
Combine the flour, sugar, butter, eggs and butterscotch pieces in a bowl and whisk together for 2 minutes or until smooth.

STEP 3
Divide the mixture between the cases, then transfer the tin to the oven and bake for 10–15 minutes. Test with a wooden toothpick, if it comes out clean, the cakes are done. Transfer the cakes to a wire rack and leave to cool completely.

STEP 4
Beat the butter until smooth, then gradually whisk in the icing sugar and butterscotch syrup. Spread the buttercream over the cakes and sprinkle with brown sugar 'sand'. Top with the seashells.

Preparation time: 1 hour 20 minutes | **Cooking time: 10–15 minutes** | **Makes: 12**

Ingredients:

110 g / 4 oz / ⅔ cup self-raising flour, sifted
110 g / 4 oz / ½ cup caster (superfine) sugar
110 g / 4 oz / ½ cup butter, softened
2 large eggs
75 g / 2 ½ oz / ½ cup white chocolate chips

To decorate:

200 g / 7 oz / 1 ⅓ cups dark chocolate, minimum 60% cocoa solids
200 ml / 7 fl. oz / ¾ cup double (heavy) cream
200 g / 7 oz / ⅔ cup ready-to-roll fondant icing
orange and brown food colouring

Chocolate owl cupcakes

Method

STEP 1
Preheat the oven to 190°C (170°C fan) / 375F / gas 5 and line a 12-hole cupcake tin with paper cases.

STEP 2
Combine the flour, sugar, butter and eggs in a bowl and whisk together for 2 minutes or until smooth. Fold in the chocolate chips, then divide the mixture between the paper cases.

STEP 3
Transfer the tin to the oven and bake for 10–15 minutes. Test with a wooden toothpick, if it comes out clean, the cakes are done. Transfer the cakes to a wire rack and leave to cool completely.

STEP 4
Finely chop the chocolate and transfer it to a mixing bowl. Heat the cream until it starts to simmer, then pour it over the chocolate and leave to stand for 30 seconds. Slowly stir the chocolate and cream together until it forms a smooth ganache.

STEP 5
Leave the ganache to cool until it's thick enough to hold its shape, then spoon it into a piping bag fitted with a large star nozzle. Pipe a swirl of ganache onto each cake.

STEP 6
Roll out half of the fondant and cut out 24 circles for the eyes, then lay them on top of the cake. Colour a third of the remaining fondant orange and make the beaks, then colour the rest brown and make the eye lids, ear feathers and pupils.

Preparation time: **1 hour 30 minutes** | Cooking time: **10–15 minutes** | Makes: **12**

Ingredients:

110 g / 4 oz / ⅔ cup self-raising flour, sifted
110 g / 4 oz / ½ cup caster (superfine) sugar
110 g / 4 oz / ½ cup butter, softened
2 large eggs
1 tsp vanilla extract

To decorate:

400 g / 14 oz / 1 ½ cups ready-to-roll fondant icing
blue, green, orange and yellow food colouring
black food colour pen

Under the sea cupcakes

Method

STEP 1
Preheat the oven to 190°C (170°C fan) / 375F / gas 5 and line a 12-hole cupcake tin with paper cases.

STEP 2
Combine the flour, sugar, butter, eggs and vanilla extract in a bowl and whisk together for 2 minutes or until smooth. Divide the mixture between the cases, then transfer the tin to the oven and bake for 10–15 minutes.

STEP 3
Test with a wooden toothpick, if it comes out clean, the cakes are done. Transfer the cakes to a wire rack and leave to cool completely.

STEP 4
Colour half of the fondant icing blue, then roll it out and cut out 12 circles a little smaller than the diameter of the top of the cakes. Wet the backs with a dab of water and smooth them onto the cakes.

STEP 5
Save a little white fondant for the eyes, then colour the rest green, orange and yellow and shape into the sea creatures and pond weed. Use the off-cuts of the blue icing to make the octopi and bubbles and add the pupils of the eyes with the black food colour pen.

Preparation time: **55 minutes** | Cooking time: **10–15 minutes** | Makes: **12**

Ingredients:

110 g / 4 oz / ⅔ cup self-raising flour, sifted
110 g / 4 oz / ½ cup caster (superfine) sugar
110 g / 4 oz / ½ cup butter, softened
2 large eggs
3 tbsp desiccated coconut

To decorate:

110 g / 4 oz / ½ cup butter, softened
225 g / 8 oz / 2 ¼ cups icing (confectioners') sugar
2 tbsp coconut milk
200 g / 7 oz / ¾ cup ready-to-roll fondant icing

Coconut starfish cupcakes

Method

STEP 1
Preheat the oven to 190°C (170°C fan) / 375F / gas 5 and line a 12-hole cupcake tin with paper cases.

STEP 2
Combine the flour, sugar, butter, eggs and desiccated coconut in a bowl and whisk together for 2 minutes or until smooth.

STEP 3
Divide the mixture between the cake cases then transfer the tin to the oven and bake for 10–15 minutes. Test with a wooden toothpick, if it comes out clean, the cakes are done. Transfer the cakes to a wire rack and leave to cool completely.

STEP 4
To make the buttercream, beat the butter until smooth then beat in the icing sugar. Use a whisk to incorporate the coconut milk, then whisk for 2 minutes or until well whipped.

STEP 5
Spoon the icing into a piping bag fitted with a large star nozzle and pipe a swirl onto each cake.

STEP 6
Roll out the fondant icing and cut out 12 starfish shapes. Prick them all over with a cocktail stick, then position on top of the cakes.

Preparation time: **1 hour 30 minutes** | Cooking time: **10–15 minutes** | Makes: **12**

Ingredients:

110 g / 4 oz / ⅔ cup self-raising flour, sifted
110 g / 4 oz / ½ cup caster (superfine) sugar
110 g / 4 oz / ½ cup butter, softened
2 large eggs
1 tsp vanilla extract

To decorate:

150 g / 5 ½ oz / 1 ½ cups icing (confectioners') sugar
200 g / 7 oz / ⅔ cup ready-to-roll fondant icing
blue, purple, pink and yellow food colouring
8 pink sugar-coated chocolates
hundreds and thousands and edible glitter

Afternoon tea cupcakes

Method

STEP 1
Preheat the oven to 190°C (170°C fan) / 375F / gas 5 and line a 12-hole cupcake tin with paper cases.

STEP 2
Combine the flour, sugar, butter, eggs and vanilla extract in a bowl and whisk together for 2 minutes or until smooth. Divide the mixture between the cases, then transfer the tin to the oven and bake for 10–15 minutes.

STEP 3
Test with a wooden toothpick, if it comes out clean, the cakes are done. Transfer the cakes to a wire rack and leave to cool completely.

STEP 4
Add a little water to the icing sugar, a few drops at a time, until it forms a smooth, spreadable icing. Reserve a little icing for the decoration, then spoon the rest onto the cakes and tap them lightly on the work surface to level it out into a smooth puddle.

STEP 5
Colour half of the fondant icing yellow, then roll it out and cut out 6 circles. Cut each circle in half and use them to form the top of the 'cupcakes'. Divide the rest of the icing into 3 pieces and colour them pink, purple and blue. Roll them out and cut out the cupcake 'cases', scoring on the detail with a sharp knife.

STEP 6
Use the reserved glacé icing to ice the fondant 'cupcakes', then decorate each one with a sugar-coated chocolate 'cherry' or some hundreds and thousands. Finish the cakes with a sprinkle of edible glitter.

Preparation time: **40 minutes** | Cooking time: **10–15 minutes** | Makes: **12**

Ingredients:

110 g / 4 oz / ⅔ cup self-raising flour, sifted
110 g / 4 oz / ½ cup caster (superfine) sugar
110 g / 4 oz / ½ cup butter, softened
2 large eggs
1 tsp vanilla extract
75 g / 2 ½ oz / ½ cup blueberries

To decorate:

110 g / 4 oz / ½ cup butter, softened
225 g / 8 oz / 2 ¼ cups icing (confectioners') sugar
2 tbsp blueberry syrup
100 g / 3 ½ oz / ⅓ cup ready-to-roll fondant icing

Blueberry seashell cupcakes

Method

STEP 1
Preheat the oven to 190°C (170°C fan) / 375F / gas 5 and line a 12-hole cupcake tin with paper cases.

STEP 2
Combine the flour, sugar, butter, eggs and vanilla extract in a bowl and whisk together for 2 minutes or until smooth. Fold in the blueberries.

STEP 3
Divide the mixture between the cake cases then transfer the tin to the oven and bake for 10–15 minutes. Test with a wooden toothpick, if it comes out clean, the cakes are done. Transfer the cakes to a wire rack and leave to cool completely.

STEP 4
To make the buttercream, beat the butter until smooth then beat in the icing sugar. Use a whisk to incorporate the blueberry syrup, then whisk for 2 minutes or until well whipped. Spread the buttercream over the cakes.

STEP 5
Divide the fondant icing into 12 balls, then press them into a seashell mould to shape. Carefully remove them from the mould and position on top of the cake.

Preparation time: **45 minutes** | Cooking time: **10–15 minutes** | Makes: **12**

Ingredients:

110 g / 4 oz / ⅔ cup self-raising flour, sifted
110 g / 4 oz / ½ cup caster (superfine) sugar
110 g / 4 oz / ½ cup butter, softened
2 large eggs
75 g / 2 ½ oz / ½ cup white chocolate chips

To decorate:

110 g / 4 oz / ½ cup butter, softened
225 g / 8 oz / 2 ¼ cups icing (confectioners') sugar
a few drops of blue food colouring
12 white chocolate snowflakes

White chocolate chip snowflake cupcakes

Method

STEP 1
Preheat the oven to 190°C (170°C fan) / 375F / gas 5 and line a 12-hole cupcake tin with paper cases.

STEP 2
Combine the flour, sugar, butter, eggs and chocolate chips in a bowl and whisk together for 2 minutes or until smooth. Divide the mixture between the cases, then transfer the tin to the oven and bake for 10–15 minutes.

STEP 3
Test with a wooden toothpick, if it comes out clean, the cakes are done. Transfer the cakes to a wire rack and leave to cool completely.

STEP 4
To make the buttercream, beat the butter until smooth then beat in the icing sugar and food colouring. Spread the buttercream over the cakes and top with the white chocolate snowflakes.

Occasion Cupcakes

Preparation time: **45 minutes** | Cooking time: **10–15 minutes** | Makes: **12**

Ingredients:

110 g / 4 oz / ⅔ cup self-raising flour, sifted
110 g / 4 oz / ½ cup caster (superfine) sugar
110 g / 4 oz / ½ cup butter, softened
1 tsp vanilla extract
2 large eggs

To decorate:

400 ml / 14 fl. oz / 1 ⅔ cups double (heavy) cream
sugar confetti to decorate

Sugar confetti cupcakes

Method

STEP 1
Preheat the oven to 190°C (170°C fan) / 375F / gas 5 and line a 12-hole cupcake tin with paper cases.

STEP 2
Measure the cake ingredients into a bowl then whisk together for 3 minutes or until smooth and light. Divide the mixture between the paper cases, then transfer the tin to the oven and bake for 10–15 minutes.

STEP 3
Test the cakes with a toothpick; if it comes out clean, the cakes are done. Transfer the cakes to a wire rack and leave to cool completely.

STEP 4
Whip the cream until it holds its shape, then spread it onto the cakes and sprinkle with sugar confetti.

Preparation time: **1 hour 30 minutes** | Cooking time: **10–15 minutes** | Makes: **12**

Ingredients:
110 g / 4 oz / ⅔ cup self-raising flour, sifted
110 g / 4 oz / ½ cup caster (superfine) sugar
110 g / 4 oz / ½ cup butter, softened
2 large eggs
1 tbsp rosewater

To decorate:
1–2 tsp rosewater
300 g / 10 ½ oz / 3 cups icing (confectioners') sugar
a few drops of pink food colouring
12 pink rose petals

Pink rose petal cupcakes

Method

STEP 1
Preheat the oven to 190°C (170°C fan) / 375F / gas 5 and line a 12-hole cupcake tin with paper cases.

STEP 2
Combine the flour, sugar, butter, eggs and rosewater in a bowl and whisk together for 2 minutes or until smooth. Divide the mixture between the cases, then transfer the tin to the oven and bake for 10–15 minutes.

STEP 3
Test with a wooden toothpick, if it comes out clean, the cakes are done. Transfer the cakes to a wire rack and leave to cool completely.

STEP 4
Add a little rosewater to the icing sugar, a few drops at a time, until it forms a smooth, thick icing. Reserve a small amount for the white dots, then colour the rest pink and spread it onto the cakes. Pipe on the white dots with a small piping bag.

STEP 5
Decorate with rose petals just before serving.

Preparation time: **1 hour 30 minutes** | **Cooking time:** **10–15 minutes** | **Makes:** **12**

Ingredients:

175 g / 6 oz / 1 ¼ cups self-raising flour, sifted
175 g / 6 oz / ¾ cup caster (superfine) sugar
175 g / 6 oz / ¾ cup butter, softened
3 large eggs
2 tsp vanilla extract

To decorate:

200 g / 7 oz / 2 cups icing (confectioners') sugar
200 g / 7 oz / ⅔ cup ready-to-roll fondant icing
pink and blue food colouring

2-tier wedding cupcakes

Method

STEP 1
Preheat the oven to 190°C (170°C fan) / 375F / gas 5 and line a standard 12-hole cupcake tin and a 12-hole mini cupcake tin with paper cases.

STEP 2
Combine the flour, sugar, butter, eggs and vanilla extract in a bowl and whisk together for 2 minutes or until smooth. Divide the mixture between the cases, then transfer the tins to the oven and bake for 10–15 minutes, removing the mini cupcakes after 8–10 minutes.

STEP 3
Test with a wooden toothpick. If it comes out clean, the cakes are done. Transfer the cakes to a wire rack and leave to cool completely.

STEP 4
Add a little water to the icing sugar, a few drops at a time, until it forms a smooth, spreadable icing. Spoon the icing onto the cakes and tap them lightly on the work surface to level it out into a smooth puddle. Sit a mini cupcake on top of each standard cupcake.

STEP 5
Colour a third of the fondant icing pink and a third blue, then roll out all three pieces. Use a small blossom plunger cutter to cut out little flowers and apply them around the base of the mini cupcakes. Add the centres with contrasting coloured icing.

STEP 6
Reroll the icing offcuts and cut them into ribbons, then roll the ribbons up to make roses. Position 3 roses on top of each cake.

Preparation time: **40 minutes** | Cooking time: **10–15 minutes** | Makes: **12**

Ingredients:

110 g / 4 oz / ⅔ cup self-raising flour, sifted
110 g / 4 oz / ½ cup caster (superfine) sugar
110 g / 4 oz / ½ cup butter, softened
2 large eggs
1 tsp vanilla extract

To decorate:

110 g / 4 oz / ½ cup butter, softened
225 g / 8 oz / 2 ¼ cups icing (confectioners') sugar
1 tsp vanilla extract
sugar pearls to decorate

Pearl wedding anniversary cupcakes

Method

STEP 1

Preheat the oven to 190°C (170°C fan) / 375F / gas 5 and line a 12-hole cupcake tin with paper cases.

STEP 2

Combine the flour, sugar, butter, eggs and vanilla extract in a bowl and whisk together for 2 minutes or until smooth.

STEP 3

Divide the mixture between the cake cases then transfer the tin to the oven and bake for 10–15 minutes. Test with a wooden toothpick, if it comes out clean, the cakes are done. Transfer the cakes to a wire rack and leave to cool completely.

STEP 4

To make the buttercream, beat the butter until smooth then beat in the icing sugar and vanilla extract. Whisk for 2 minutes or until well whipped.

STEP 5

Spread the buttercream onto the cakes, then dip the outside edge in sugar pearls to coat.

Preparation time: 40 minutes | **Cooking time: 10–15 minutes** | **Makes: 12**

Ingredients:

110 g / 4 oz / ⅔ cup self-raising flour, sifted
110 g / 4 oz / ½ cup caster (superfine) sugar
110 g / 4 oz / ½ cup butter, softened
2 large eggs
1 tsp vanilla extract

To decorate:

110 g / 4 oz / ½ cup butter, softened
225 g / 8 oz / 2 ¼ cups icing (confectioners') sugar, plus extra for dusting
2 tbsp milk
1 tsp vanilla extract
3 tbsp edible silver balls

Silver wedding cupcakes

Method

STEP 1
Preheat the oven to 190°C (170°C fan) / 375F / gas 5 and line a 12-hole cupcake tin with paper cases.

STEP 2
Combine the flour, sugar, butter, eggs and vanilla extract in a bowl and whisk together for 2 minutes or until smooth.

STEP 3
Divide the mixture between the cake cases then transfer the tin to the oven and bake for 10–15 minutes. Test with a wooden toothpick, if it comes out clean, the cakes are done. Transfer the cakes to a wire rack and leave to cool completely.

STEP 4
To make the buttercream, beat the butter until smooth then beat in the icing sugar. Use a whisk to incorporate the milk and vanilla extract, then whisk for 2 minutes or until well whipped.

STEP 5
Spoon the icing into a piping bag fitted with a large star nozzle and pipe a swirl on top of each cake. Decorate with the silver balls and finish with a dusting of icing sugar.

Preparation time: **40 minutes** | Cooking time: **10–15 minutes** | Makes: **12**

Ingredients:

110 g / 4 oz / ⅔ cup self-raising flour, sifted
110 g / 4 oz / ½ cup caster (superfine) sugar
110 g / 4 oz / ½ cup butter, softened
2 large eggs
½ tsp rosewater
½ tsp orange flower water

To decorate:

110 g / 4 oz / ½ cup butter, softened
225 g / 8 oz / 2 ¼ cups icing (confectioners') sugar, plus extra for dusting
2 tbsp milk
½ tsp rosewater
½ tsp orange flower water
100 g / 3 ½ oz / ⅓ cup yellow ready-to-roll fondant icing

Blossom cupcakes

Method

STEP 1
Preheat the oven to 190°C (170°C fan) / 375F / gas 5 and line a 12-hole cupcake tin with paper cases.

STEP 2
Combine the flour, sugar, butter, eggs and flower waters in a bowl and whisk together for 2 minutes or until smooth.

STEP 3
Divide the mixture between the cake cases then transfer the tin to the oven and bake for 10–15 minutes. Test with a wooden toothpick, if it comes out clean, the cakes are done. Transfer the cakes to a wire rack and leave to cool completely.

STEP 4
To make the buttercream, beat the butter until smooth then beat in the icing sugar. Use a whisk to incorporate the milk and flower waters, then whisk for 2 minutes or until well whipped. Reserve a quarter of the icing for the flower centres and spread the rest over the cakes.

STEP 5
Roll out the yellow fondant and use different sized blossom plunger cutters to cut out the flowers, applying them directly onto the surface of the cakes.

STEP 6
Put the reserved buttercream into a piping bag fitted with a small plain nozzle and pipe in the centres of the flowers.

Preparation time: **40 minutes** | Cooking time: **10–15 minutes** | Makes: **12**

Ingredients:

110 g / 4 oz / ⅔ cup self-raising flour, sifted
110 g / 4 oz / ½ cup caster (superfine) sugar
110 g / 4 oz / ½ cup butter, softened
2 large eggs
1 lemon, zest finely grated

To decorate:

110 g / 4 oz / ½ cup butter, softened
225 g / 8 oz / 2 ¼ cups icing (confectioners') sugar, plus extra for dusting
1 tbsp lemon juice
sugar pearls to decorate

Lemon pearl cupcakes

Method

STEP 1
Preheat the oven to 190°C (170°C fan) / 375F / gas 5 and line a 12-hole cupcake tin with paper cases.

STEP 2
Combine the flour, sugar, butter, eggs and lemon zest in a bowl and whisk together for 2 minutes or until smooth.

STEP 3
Divide the mixture between the cake cases then transfer the tin to the oven and bake for 10–15 minutes. Test with a wooden toothpick, if it comes out clean, the cakes are done. Transfer the cakes to a wire rack and leave to cool completely.

STEP 4
To make the buttercream, beat the butter until smooth then beat in the icing sugar. Use a whisk to incorporate the lemon juice, then whisk for 2 minutes or until well whipped.

STEP 5
Spoon the icing into a piping bag fitted with a large star nozzle and pipe a swirl on top of each cake. Finish with a sprinkle of sugar pearls.

Preparation time: **45 minutes** | Cooking time: **10–15 minutes** | Makes: **12**

Ingredients:

110 g / 4 oz / ⅔ cup self-raising flour, sifted
110 g / 4 oz / ½ cup caster (superfine) sugar
110 g / 4 oz / ½ cup butter, softened
2 large eggs
2 tbsp unsweetened cocoa powder

To decorate:

100 g / 3 ½ oz / ½ cup butter, softened
200 g / 7 oz / 2 cups icing (confectioners') sugar
2 tbsp cocoa powder
1 tbsp milk
6 chocolate flakes, broken into pieces
36 chocolate mini eggs

Easter nest cupcakes

Method

STEP 1
Preheat the oven to 190°C (170°C fan) / 375F / gas 5 and line a 12-hole cupcake tin with paper cases.

STEP 2
Combine the flour, sugar, butter, eggs and cocoa powder in a bowl and whisk together for 2 minutes or until smooth.

STEP 3
Divide the mixture between the cases, then transfer the tin to the oven and bake for 10–15 minutes. Test with a wooden toothpick, if it comes out clean, the cakes are done. Transfer the cakes to a wire rack and leave to cool completely.

STEP 4
Beat the butter until smooth, then gradually whisk in the icing sugar, cocoa powder and milk.

STEP 5
Spoon the mixture into a piping bag, fitted with a large star nozzle, and pipe a swirl of icing on top of each cake.

STEP 6
Arrange the pieces of flake into a nest shape on top of the cakes and decorate with the mini eggs.

Preparation time: **1 hour 30 minutes** | **Cooking time:** **10–15 minutes** | **Makes:** **12**

Ingredients:

110 g / 4 oz / ⅔ cup self-raising flour, sifted
110 g / 4 oz / ½ cup caster (superfine) sugar
110 g / 4 oz / ½ cup butter, softened
2 large eggs
2 tbsp unsweetened cocoa powder

To decorate:

100 g / 3 ½ oz / ½ cup butter, softened
200 g / 7 oz / 2 cups icing (confectioners') sugar
2 tbsp cocoa powder
1 tbsp milk
300 g / 10 ½ oz / 1 cup ready-to-roll fondant icing
pink, purple, orange and green food colouring
edible glitter for sprinkling

Fondant flower cupcakes

Method

STEP 1
Preheat the oven to 190°C (170°C fan) / 375F / gas 5 and line a 12-hole cupcake tin with paper cases.

STEP 2
Combine the flour, sugar, butter, eggs and cocoa powder in a bowl and whisk together for 2 minutes or until smooth.

STEP 3
Divide the mixture between the cases, then transfer the tin to the oven and bake for 10–15 minutes. Test with a wooden toothpick, if it comes out clean, the cakes are done. Transfer the cakes to a wire rack and leave to cool completely.

STEP 4
Beat the butter until smooth, then gradually whisk in the icing sugar, cocoa powder and milk. Spoon the mixture into a piping bag, fitted with a large star nozzle, and pipe stars of the icing all over the top of each cake.

STEP 5
Divide the fondant icing into 5 pieces and colour 4 of them with the food colourings. Roll out each piece of fondant and cut out different size hearts, leaves, butterflies and stars, adding contrasting coloured centres to each flower.

STEP 6
Arrange the fondant shapes on top of the cakes to completely cover the surface, then sprinkle with a little edible glitter.

Preparation time: **50 minutes** | Cooking time: **10–15 minutes** | Makes: **12**

Ingredients:
110 g / 4 oz / ⅔ cup self-raising flour, sifted
110 g / 4 oz / ½ cup caster (superfine) sugar
110 g / 4 oz / ½ cup butter, softened
2 large eggs
1 tsp vanilla extract

To decorate:
110 g / 4 oz / ½ cup butter, softened
225 g / 8 oz / 2 ¼ cups icing (confectioners') sugar
2 tbsp milk
1 tsp vanilla extract
36 sugar flowers
mini gift wrap bunting
24 cocktail sticks

Bunting cupcakes

Method

STEP 1
Preheat the oven to 190°C (170°C fan) / 375F / gas 5 and line a 12-hole cupcake tin with paper cases.

STEP 2
Combine the flour, sugar, butter, eggs and vanilla extract in a bowl and whisk together for 2 minutes or until smooth.

STEP 3
Divide the mixture between the cake cases then transfer the tin to the oven and bake for 10–15 minutes. Test with a wooden toothpick, if it comes out clean, the cakes are done. Transfer the cakes to a wire rack and leave to cool completely.

STEP 4
To make the buttercream, beat the butter until smooth then beat in the icing sugar. Use a whisk to incorporate the milk and vanilla extract, then whisk for 2 minutes or until well whipped.

STEP 5
Spoon the icing into a piping bag fitted with a large star nozzle. Pipe a big swirl on top of each cake and top with the sugar flowers.

STEP 6
Cut the bunting into strings of 3 then attach the ends to the cocktail stick 'poles' and assemble them onto the cakes.

Preparation time: **40 minutes** | Cooking time: **10–15 minutes** | Makes: **12**

Ingredients:

110 g / 4 oz / ⅔ cup self-raising flour, sifted
110 g / 4 oz / ½ cup caster (superfine) sugar
110 g / 4 oz / ½ cup butter, softened
2 large eggs
1 tsp vanilla extract

To decorate:

110 g / 4 oz / ½ cup butter, softened
225 g / 8 oz / 2 ¼ cups icing (confectioners') sugar, plus extra for dusting
2 tbsp strawberry syrup
sugar pearls to decorate

Strawberry pearl cupcakes

Method

STEP 1
Preheat the oven to 190°C (170°C fan) / 375F / gas 5 and line a 12-hole cupcake tin with paper cases.

STEP 2
Combine the flour, sugar, butter, eggs and vanilla extract in a bowl and whisk together for 2 minutes or until smooth.

STEP 3
Divide the mixture between the cake cases then transfer the tin to the oven and bake for 10–15 minutes. Test with a wooden toothpick, if it comes out clean, the cakes are done. Transfer the cakes to a wire rack and leave to cool completely.

STEP 4
To make the buttercream, beat the butter until smooth then beat in the icing sugar. Use a whisk to incorporate the strawberry syrup, then whisk for 2 minutes or until well whipped.

STEP 5
Spread the buttercream onto the cakes and decorate with sugar pearls.

Preparation time: 40 minutes | Cooking time: 10–15 minutes | Makes: 12

Ingredients:
110 g / 4 oz / ⅔ cup self-raising flour, sifted
110 g / 4 oz / ½ cup caster (superfine) sugar
110 g / 4 oz / ½ cup butter, softened
2 large eggs
1 tsp rosewater

To decorate:
110 g / 4 oz / ½ cup butter, softened
225 g / 8 oz / 2 ¼ cups icing (confectioners') sugar, plus extra for dusting
1 tbsp rosewater
a few drops of pink food colouring
clear sugar crystal sprinkles to decorate

Rose sprinkle cupcakes

Method

STEP 1
Preheat the oven to 190°C (170°C fan) / 375F / gas 5 and line a 12-hole cupcake tin with paper cases.

STEP 2
Combine the flour, sugar, butter, eggs and rosewater in a bowl and whisk together for 2 minutes or until smooth.

STEP 3
Divide the mixture between the cake cases then transfer the tin to the oven and bake for 10–15 minutes. Test with a wooden toothpick, if it comes out clean, the cakes are done. Transfer the cakes to a wire rack and leave to cool completely.

STEP 4
To make the buttercream, beat the butter until smooth then beat in the icing sugar. Use a whisk to incorporate the rosewater and food colouring, then whisk for 2 minutes or until well whipped.

STEP 5
Spread the buttercream over the cakes and sprinkle with sugar crystals.

Preparation time: **40 minutes** | Cooking time: **10–15 minutes** | Makes: **12**

Ingredients:

110 g / 4 oz / ⅔ cup self-raising flour, sifted
110 g / 4 oz / ½ cup caster (superfine) sugar
110 g / 4 oz / ½ cup butter, softened
2 large eggs
1 tsp vanilla extract

To decorate:

110 g / 4 oz / ½ cup butter, softened
225 g / 8 oz / 2 ¼ cups icing (confectioners') sugar, plus extra for dusting
a few drops of green food colouring
sugar daisies to decorate

Daisy meadow cupcakes

Method

STEP 1
Preheat the oven to 190°C (170°C fan) / 375F / gas 5 and line a 12-hole cupcake tin with paper cases.

STEP 2
Combine the flour, sugar, butter, eggs and vanilla extract in a bowl and whisk together for 2 minutes or until smooth.

STEP 3
Divide the mixture between the cake cases then transfer the tin to the oven and bake for 10–15 minutes. Test with a wooden toothpick, if it comes out clean, the cakes are done. Transfer the cakes to a wire rack and leave to cool completely.

STEP 4
To make the buttercream, beat the butter until smooth then beat in the icing sugar and food colouring. Whisk for 2 minutes or until well whipped.

STEP 5
Spread the buttercream onto the cakes and decorate with sugar daisies.

Preparation time: **40 minutes** | Cooking time: **10–15 minutes** | Makes: **12**

Ingredients:

110 g / 4 oz / ⅔ cup self-raising flour, sifted
110 g / 4 oz / ½ cup caster (superfine) sugar
110 g / 4 oz / ½ cup butter, softened
2 large eggs
1 tsp rosewater

To decorate:

110 g / 4 oz / ½ cup butter, softened
225 g / 8 oz / 2 ¼ cups icing (confectioners') sugar, plus extra for dusting
2 tbsp milk
1 tsp rosewater
50 g / 1 ¾ oz / ¼ cup pink ready-to-roll fondant icing

Rose petal cupcakes

Method

STEP 1
Preheat the oven to 190°C (170°C fan) / 375F / gas 5 and line a 12-hole cupcake tin with paper cases.

STEP 2
Combine the flour, sugar, butter, eggs and rosewater in a bowl and whisk together for 2 minutes or until smooth.

STEP 3
Divide the mixture between the cake cases then transfer the tin to the oven and bake for 10–15 minutes. Test with a wooden toothpick, if it comes out clean, the cakes are done. Transfer the cakes to a wire rack and leave to cool completely.

STEP 4
To make the buttercream, beat the butter until smooth then beat in the icing sugar. Use a whisk to incorporate the milk and rosewater, then whisk for 2 minutes or until well whipped.

STEP 5
Spoon the icing into a piping bag fitted with a large star nozzle and pipe it onto the cakes.

STEP 6
To make the rose petals, roll a small piece of pink fondant into a ball, then flatten it between your thumb and forefinger, thinning round the edge as you go. Lay a petal on top of each cake.

Preparation time: 1 hour 30 minutes | **Cooking time:** 10–15 minutes | **Makes:** 12

Ingredients:

110 g / 4 oz / ⅔ cup self-raising flour, sifted
110 g / 4 oz / ½ cup caster (superfine) sugar
110 g / 4 oz / ½ cup butter, softened
2 large eggs
1 tsp vanilla extract

To decorate:

200 g / 7 oz / ⅔ cup ready-to-roll fondant icing
purple food colouring
300 g / 10 ½ oz / 3 cups icing (confectioners') sugar

Purple butterfly cupcakes

Method

STEP 1
Colour a third of the fondant icing purple and leave the rest white. Roll out both pieces then use a butterfly plunger cutter to cut out 36 butterflies. Fold a piece of card in an 'M' shape and lay the butterflies in the valley down the middle. Leave to set and harden overnight.

STEP 2
Preheat the oven to 190°C (170°C fan) / 375F / gas 5 and line a 12-hole cupcake tin with paper cases.

STEP 3
Combine the flour, sugar, butter, eggs and vanilla extract in a bowl and whisk together for 2 minutes or until smooth. Divide the mixture between the cases, then transfer the tin to the oven and bake for 10–15 minutes.

STEP 4
Test with a wooden toothpick, if it comes out clean, the cakes are done. Transfer the cakes to a wire rack and leave to cool completely.

STEP 5
Add a little water to the icing sugar, a few drops at a time, until it forms a smooth, spreadable icing. Reserve a little icing for decoration, then spoon the rest onto the cakes.

STEP 6
Position the butterflies on top of the cakes and pipe on the reserved glacé icing to make the bodies.

STEP 7
Leave to set.

Preparation time: **1 hour 30 minutes** | **Cooking time:** **10–15 minutes** | **Makes:** **12**

Ingredients:

110 g / 4 oz / ⅔ cup self-raising flour, sifted
110 g / 4 oz / ½ cup caster (superfine) sugar
110 g / 4 oz / ½ cup butter, softened
2 large eggs
1 tbsp rosewater

To decorate:

1–2 tsp rosewater
300 g / 10 ½ oz / 3 cups icing (confectioners') sugar
12 fondant roses with leaves

Rosewater icing cupcakes

Method

STEP 1
Preheat the oven to 190°C (170°C fan) / 375F / gas 5 and line a 12-hole cupcake tin with paper cases.

STEP 2
Combine the flour, sugar, butter, eggs and rosewater in a bowl and whisk together for 2 minutes or until smooth. Divide the mixture between the cases, then transfer the tin to the oven and bake for 10–15 minutes.

STEP 3
Test with a wooden toothpick, if it comes out clean, the cakes are done. Transfer the cakes to a wire rack and leave to cool completely.

STEP 4
Add a little rosewater to the icing sugar, a few drops at a time, until it forms a smooth, thick icing, then spoon it onto the cakes.

STEP 5
Position the roses on top and leave for 2 hours for the icing to set.

Preparation time: **40 minutes** | Cooking time: **10–15 minutes** | Makes: **12**

Ingredients:

110 g / 4 oz / ⅔ cup self-raising flour, sifted
110 g / 4 oz / ½ cup caster (superfine) sugar
110 g / 4 oz / ½ cup butter, softened
2 large eggs
1 tsp rosewater

To decorate:

110 g / 4 oz / ½ cup butter, softened
225 g / 8 oz / 2 ¼ cups icing (confectioners') sugar
2 tbsp milk
1 tsp rosewater
sugar pearls and red sugar hearts to decorate

Valentines cupcakes

Method

STEP 1
Preheat the oven to 190°C (170°C fan) / 375F / gas 5 and line a 12-hole cupcake tin with paper cases.

STEP 2
Combine the flour, sugar, butter, eggs and rosewater in a bowl and whisk together for 2 minutes or until smooth.

STEP 3
Divide the mixture between the cake cases then transfer the tin to the oven and bake for 10–15 minutes. Test with a wooden toothpick, if it comes out clean, the cakes are done. Transfer the cakes to a wire rack and leave to cool completely.

STEP 4
To make the buttercream, beat the butter until smooth then beat in the icing sugar. Use a whisk to incorporate the milk and rosewater, then whisk for 2 minutes or until well whipped.

STEP 5
Spoon the icing into a piping bag fitted with a large star nozzle and pipe a big swirl on top of each cake. Decorate with the sugar pearls and hearts.

Preparation time: 40 minutes | Cooking time: 10–15 minutes | Makes: 12

Ingredients:

110 g / 4 oz / ⅔ cup self-raising flour, sifted
110 g / 4 oz / ½ cup caster (superfine) sugar
110 g / 4 oz / ½ cup butter, softened
2 large eggs
1 lemon, zest finely grated

To decorate:

110 g / 4 oz / ½ cup butter, softened
225 g / 8 oz / 2 ¼ cups icing (confectioners') sugar, plus extra for dusting
1 tbsp lemon juice
yellow, orange and white hundreds and thousands
12 sugar flowers

Lemon pollen cupcakes

Method

STEP 1
Preheat the oven to 190°C (170°C fan) / 375F / gas 5 and line a 12-hole cupcake tin with paper cases.

STEP 2
Combine the flour, sugar, butter, eggs and lemon zest in a bowl and whisk together for 2 minutes or until smooth.

STEP 3
Divide the mixture between the cake cases then transfer the tin to the oven and bake for 10–15 minutes. Test with a wooden toothpick, if it comes out clean, the cakes are done. Transfer the cakes to a wire rack and leave to cool completely.

STEP 4
To make the buttercream, beat the butter until smooth then beat in the icing sugar. Use a whisk to incorporate the lemon juice, then whisk for 2 minutes or until well whipped.

STEP 5
Spread the buttercream over the cakes, then dip the edges in hundreds and thousands to coat. Position a sugar flower on top of each one and sprinkle a few more hundreds and thousands in the centre.

Preparation time: **40 minutes** | Cooking time: **10–15 minutes** | Makes: **12**

Ingredients:

110 g / 4 oz / ⅔ cup self-raising flour, sifted
110 g / 4 oz / ½ cup caster (superfine) sugar
110 g / 4 oz / ½ cup butter, softened
2 large eggs
1 lemon, zest finely grated

To decorate:

110 g / 4 oz / ½ cup butter, softened
225 g / 8 oz / 2 ¼ cups icing (confectioners') sugar, plus extra for dusting
1 tbsp lemon juice
100 g / 3 ½ oz / ⅓ cup yellow ready-to-roll fondant icing

Lemon lace cupcakes

Method

STEP 1
Preheat the oven to 190°C (170°C fan) / 375F / gas 5 and line a 12-hole cupcake tin with paper cases.

STEP 2
Combine the flour, sugar, butter, eggs and lemon zest in a bowl and whisk together for 2 minutes or until smooth.

STEP 3
Divide the mixture between the cake cases then transfer the tin to the oven and bake for 10–15 minutes. Test with a wooden toothpick, if it comes out clean, the cakes are done. Transfer the cakes to a wire rack and leave to cool completely.

STEP 4
To make the buttercream, beat the butter until smooth then beat in the icing sugar. Use a whisk to incorporate the lemon juice, then whisk for 2 minutes or until well whipped. Spread a third of the icing over the top of the cakes.

STEP 5
Spoon the rest of the buttercream into a piping bag fitted with a large star nozzle and pipe a swirl on top of each cake.

STEP 6
Roll out the yellow fondant and use a lace embossing tool to press a pattern into the top. Cut out 12 circles and lay one on top of each cake.

Special Treats

Preparation time: **45 minutes** | Cooking time: **10–15 minutes** | Makes: **12**

Ingredients:

110 g / 4 oz / ⅔ cup self-raising flour, sifted
110 g / 4 oz / ½ cup caster (superfine) sugar
110 g / 4 oz / ½ cup butter, softened
1 tsp vanilla extract
2 large eggs

To decorate:

400 ml / 14 fl. oz / 1 ⅔ cups double (heavy) cream
3 large strawberries, quartered
36 blueberries
36 raspberries
strawberry syrup for drizzling

Berries and cream cupcakes

Method

STEP 1
Preheat the oven to 190°C (170°C fan) / 375F / gas 5 and line a 12-hole cupcake tin with paper cases.

STEP 2
Measure the cake ingredients into a bowl then whisk together for 3 minutes or until smooth and light. Divide the mixture between the paper cases, then transfer the tin to the oven and bake for 10–15 minutes.

STEP 3
Test the cakes with a toothpick; if it comes out clean, the cakes are done. Transfer the cakes to a wire rack and leave to cool completely.

STEP 4
Whip the cream until it holds its shape, then spoon it into a piping bag fitted with a large star nozzle and pipe a swirl on top of each cake.

STEP 5
Arrange the berries on top of the cakes and drizzle with a little strawberry syrup.

Preparation time: 1 hour 10 minutes | **Cooking time:** 10–15 minutes | **Makes:** 12

Ingredients:
110 g / 4 oz / ⅔ cup self-raising flour, sifted
110 g / 4 oz / ½ cup caster (superfine) sugar
110 g / 4 oz / ½ cup butter, softened
2 large eggs
1 tsp vanilla extract
75 g / 2 ½ oz / ½ cup white chocolate chips

To decorate:
200 g / 7 oz / 1 ⅓ cups milk chocolate
200 ml / 7 fl. oz / ¾ cup double (heavy) cream
100 g / 3 ½ oz / ⅔ cup dark chocolate (minimum 60% cocoa solids)
12 fresh cherries
white chocolate vermicelli to sprinkle

Chocolate cherry treat cupcakes

Method

STEP 1
Preheat the oven to 190°C (170°C fan) / 375F / gas 5 and line a 12-hole cupcake tin with paper cases.

STEP 2
Combine the flour, sugar, butter, eggs and vanilla extract in a bowl and whisk together for 2 minutes or until smooth. Fold in the chocolate chips, then divide the mixture between the paper cases.

STEP 3
Transfer the tin to the oven and bake for 10–15 minutes. Test with a wooden toothpick, if it comes out clean, the cakes are done. Transfer the cakes to a wire rack and leave to cool completely.

STEP 4
Finely chop the milk chocolate and transfer it to a mixing bowl. Heat the cream until it starts to simmer, then pour it over the chocolate and leave to stand for 30 seconds. Slowly stir the chocolate and cream until it forms a smooth ganache.

STEP 5
Leave the ganache to cool until it's thick enough to hold its shape, then spoon it into a piping bag fitted with a large plain nozzle. Pipe a swirl of ganache onto each cake.

STEP 6
Melt the dark chocolate and drizzle it over the ganache, then top each one with a cherry and a sprinkle of white chocolate vermicelli.

Preparation time: **45 minutes** | Cooking time: **10–15 minutes** | Makes: **12**

Ingredients:

110 g / 4 oz / ⅔ cup self-raising flour, sifted
110 g / 4 oz / ½ cup caster (superfine) sugar
110 g / 4 oz / ½ cup butter, softened
1 tsp vanilla extract
2 large eggs

To decorate:

400 ml / 14 fl. oz / 1 ⅔ cups double (heavy) cream
36 raspberries
raspberry syrup for drizzling

Raspberry drizzle cupcakes

Method

STEP 1
Preheat the oven to 190°C (170°C fan) / 375F / gas 5 and line a 12-hole cupcake tin with paper cases.

STEP 2
Measure the cake ingredients into a bowl then whisk together for 3 minutes or until smooth and light. Divide the mixture between the paper cases, then transfer the tin to the oven and bake for 10–15 minutes.

STEP 3
Test the cakes with a toothpick; if it comes out clean, the cakes are done. Transfer the cakes to a wire rack and leave to cool completely.

STEP 4
Whip the cream until it holds its shape, then spoon it into a piping bag fitted with a large star nozzle and pipe a swirl on top of each cake.

STEP 5
Arrange the raspberries on top of the cakes and drizzle with a little raspberry syrup.

Preparation time: **40 minutes** | Cooking time: **10–15 minutes** | Makes: **12**

Ingredients:

110 g / 4 oz / ⅔ cup self-raising flour, sifted
110 g / 4 oz / ½ cup caster (superfine) sugar
110 g / 4 oz / ½ cup butter, softened
2 large eggs
1 tsp vanilla extract

To decorate:

110 g / 4 oz / ½ cup butter, softened
225 g / 8 oz / 2 ¼ cups icing (confectioners') sugar, plus extra for dusting
3 tbsp strawberry syrup
12 strawberries

Strawberry ripple cupcakes

Method

STEP 1
Preheat the oven to 190°C (170°C fan) / 375F / gas 5 and line a 12-hole cupcake tin with paper cases.

STEP 2
Combine the flour, sugar, butter, eggs and vanilla extract in a bowl and whisk together for 2 minutes or until smooth.

STEP 3
Divide the mixture between the cake cases then transfer the tin to the oven and bake for 10–15 minutes. Test with a wooden toothpick, if it comes out clean, the cakes are done. Transfer the cakes to a wire rack and leave to cool completely.

STEP 4
To make the buttercream, beat the butter until smooth then beat in the icing sugar. Fold through the strawberry syrup to create a rippled effect, then spoon it onto the cakes.

STEP 5
Top each cake with a strawberry and a light dusting of icing sugar.

Preparation time: **40 minutes** | Cooking time: **10–15 minutes** | Makes: **12**

Ingredients:

110 g / 4 oz / ⅔ cup self-raising flour, sifted
110 g / 4 oz / ½ cup caster (superfine) sugar
110 g / 4 oz / ½ cup butter, softened
2 large eggs
1 tsp vanilla extract

To decorate:

110 g / 4 oz / ½ cup butter, softened
225 g / 8 oz / 2 ¼ cups icing (confectioners') sugar, plus extra for dusting
2 tbsp milk
1 tsp vanilla extract
75 g / 2 ½ oz / 1 ¼ cups mini marshmallows

Marshmallow cupcakes

Method

STEP 1
Preheat the oven to 190°C (170°C fan) / 375F / gas 5 and line a 12-hole cupcake tin with paper cases.

STEP 2
Combine the flour, sugar, butter, eggs and vanilla extract in a bowl and whisk together for 2 minutes or until smooth.

STEP 3
Divide the mixture between the cake cases then transfer the tin to the oven and bake for 10–15 minutes. Test with a wooden toothpick, if it comes out clean, the cakes are done. Transfer the cakes to a wire rack and leave to cool completely.

STEP 4
To make the buttercream, beat the butter until smooth then beat in the icing sugar. Use a whisk to incorporate the milk and vanilla extract, then whisk for 2 minutes or until well whipped.

STEP 5
Spread the buttercream onto the cakes and top with the marshmallows.

Preparation time: **45 minutes** | Cooking time: **10–15 minutes** | Makes: **12**

Ingredients:

110 g / 4 oz / ⅔ cup self-raising flour, sifted
110 g / 4 oz / ½ cup caster (superfine) sugar
110 g / 4 oz / ½ cup butter, softened
1 tsp vanilla extract
2 large eggs

To decorate:

4 tbsp raspberry jam (jelly)
400 ml / 14 fl. oz / 1 ⅔ cups double (heavy) cream
2 meringue nests, broken into pieces
36 raspberries
icing (confectioners') sugar for dusting

Raspberry mess cupcakes

Method

STEP 1
Preheat the oven to 190°C (170°C fan) / 375F / gas 5 and line a 12-hole cupcake tin with paper cases.

STEP 2
Measure the cake ingredients into a bowl then whisk together for 3 minutes or until smooth and light. Divide the mixture between the paper cases, then transfer the tin to the oven and bake for 10–15 minutes.

STEP 3
Test the cakes with a toothpick; if it comes out clean, the cakes are done. Transfer the cakes to a wire rack and leave to cool completely.

STEP 4
Cut a cone out of the centre of each cake and fill with jam, then replace the cone of cake.

STEP 5
Whip the cream until it holds its shape, then spoon a little onto each cake. Top each cake with a few pieces of meringue and 3 raspberries, then dust lightly with icing sugar.

Preparation time: 1 hour | Cooking time: **15–20 minutes** | Makes: 12

Ingredients:

110 g / 4 oz / ⅔ cup self-raising flour, sifted
110 g / 4 oz / ½ cup caster (superfine) sugar
110 g / 4 oz / ½ cup butter, softened
2 large eggs
1 lemon, zest finely grated

To decorate:

225 g / 8 oz / 1 cup lemon curd
4 large egg whites
110g / 4 oz / 1 cup caster (superfine) sugar

Lemon meringue cupcakes

Method

STEP 1
Preheat the oven to 190°C (170°C fan) / 375F / gas 5 and line a 12-hole cupcake tin with paper cases.

STEP 2
Combine the flour, sugar, butter, eggs and lemon zest in a bowl and whisk together for 2 minutes or until smooth.

STEP 3
Divide the mixture between the paper cases, then transfer the tin to the oven and bake for 10–15 minutes. Test with a wooden toothpick, if it comes out clean, the cakes are done.

STEP 4
Use a teaspoon to make a hollow in the centre of each cake and fill with lemon curd.

STEP 5
To make the meringue topping, whisk the egg whites until stiff, then gradually whisk in half the sugar until the mixture is very shiny. Fold in the remaining sugar then spoon the meringue into a large piping bag fitted with a plain nozzle.

STEP 6
Pipe the meringue onto the cakes, then return the tin to the oven for 5 minutes or until the topping is lightly toasted. Serve warm or leave to cool to room temperature.

Preparation time: **1 hour 10 minutes** | Cooking time: **10–15 minutes** | Makes: **12**

Ingredients:
110 g / 4 oz / ⅔ cup self-raising flour, sifted
2 tbsp unsweetened cocoa powder
110 g / 4 oz / ½ cup caster (superfine) sugar
110 g / 4 oz / ½ cup butter, softened
2 large eggs
75 g / 2 ½ oz / ⅓ cup dried cherries
75 g / 2 ½ oz / ½ cup almonds, chopped

To decorate:
300 g / 10 ½ oz / 2 cups dark chocolate, minimum 60% cocoa solids
200 ml / 7 fl. oz / ⅔ cup double (heavy) cream
75 g / 2 ½ oz / 1 ¼ cups mini marshmallows
75 g / 2 ½ oz / ⅓ cup dried cherries
75 g / 2 ½ oz / ½ cup almonds

Rocky road cupcakes

Method

STEP 1
Preheat the oven to 190°C (170°C fan) / 375F / gas 5 and line a 12-hole cupcake tin with paper cases.

STEP 2
Combine the flour, cocoa, sugar, butter and eggs in a bowl and whisk together for 2 minutes or until smooth. Fold in the cherries and chopped almonds, then divide the mixture between the paper cases.

STEP 3
Transfer the tin to the oven and bake for 10–15 minutes. Test with a wooden toothpick, if it comes out clean, the cakes are done. Transfer the cakes to a wire rack and leave to cool completely.

STEP 4
Finely chop 200 g / 7 oz / 1 ⅓ cups of the chocolate and transfer it to a mixing bowl. Heat the cream until it starts to simmer, then pour it over the chocolate and leave to stand for 30 seconds. Slowly stir the chocolate and cream together until it forms a smooth ganache.

STEP 5
Leave the ganache to cool until it's thick enough to hold its shape, then spoon it into a piping bag fitted with a large star nozzle. Pipe a swirl of ganache onto each cake.

STEP 6
Top the cakes with the marshmallows, cherries and almonds, then melt the rest of the chocolate and drizzle it over the top.

Preparation time: **1 hour 20 minutes** | Cooking time: **10–15 minutes** | Makes: **12**

Ingredients:

110 g / 4 oz / ⅔ cup self-raising flour, sifted
110 g / 4 oz / ½ cup caster (superfine) sugar
110 g / 4 oz / ½ cup butter, softened
2 large eggs
75 g / 2 ½ oz / ⅓ cup glacé cherries, chopped

To decorate:

3 tbsp cherry jam (jelly), sieved
300 g / 10 ½ oz / 1 cup ready-to-roll fondant icing
red and green food colouring
150 g / 5 ½ oz / 1 ½ cups icing (confectioners') sugar

Fondant cherry cupcakes

Method

STEP 1
Preheat the oven to 190°C (170°C fan) / 375F / gas 5 and line a 12-hole cupcake tin with paper cases.

STEP 2
Combine the flour, sugar, butter, eggs and cherries in a bowl and whisk together for 2 minutes or until smooth. Divide the mixture between the cases, then transfer the tin to the oven and bake for 10–15 minutes.

STEP 3
Test with a wooden toothpick, if it comes out clean, the cakes are done. Transfer the cakes to a wire rack and leave to cool completely.

STEP 4
Roll out the fondant icing and cut out 12 scallop-edged circles a little smaller in diameter than the top of the cakes. Spread the top of each cake with cherry jam, then smooth the icing on top.

STEP 5
Colour the fondant off-cuts red, then roll them into 24 'cherries' and attach the to the cakes with a dab of water.

STEP 6
Add a little water to the icing sugar, a few drops at a time, until it forms a smooth, spreadable icing, then colour it pale green. Spoon it into a piping bag fitted with a small plain nozzle and pipe the cherry stalks onto the cakes and a row of dots around the edges.

Preparation time: **45 minutes** | Cooking time: **10–15 minutes** | Makes: **12**

Ingredients:

110 g / 4 oz / ⅔ cup self-raising flour, sifted
110 g / 4 oz / ½ cup caster (superfine) sugar
110 g / 4 oz / ½ cup butter, softened
1 tsp vanilla extract
2 large eggs

To decorate:

4 tbsp strawberry jam (jelly)
400 ml / 14 fl. oz / 1 ⅔ cups double (heavy) cream
6 large strawberries, halved
icing (confectioners') sugar for dusting

Strawberries and cream cupcakes

Method

STEP 1
Preheat the oven to 190°C (170°C fan) / 375F / gas 5 and line a 12-hole cupcake tin with paper cases.

STEP 2
Measure the cake ingredients into a bowl then whisk together for 3 minutes or until smooth and light. Divide the mixture between the paper cases, then transfer the tin to the oven and bake for 10–15 minutes.

STEP 3
Test the cakes with a toothpick; if it comes out clean, the cakes are done. Transfer the cakes to a wire rack and leave to cool completely.

STEP 4
Cut a cone out of the centre of each cake and fill with strawberry jam, then replace the cone of cake.

STEP 5
Whip the cream until it holds its shape, then spoon it into a piping bag fitted with a large plain nozzle and pipe a swirl on top of each cake. Top each cake with half a strawberry and dust lightly with icing sugar.

Preparation time: **1 hour 10 minutes** | **Cooking time:** **10–15 minutes** | **Makes:** **12**

Ingredients:

110 g / 4 oz / ⅔ cup self-raising flour, sifted
110 g / 4 oz / ½ cup caster (superfine) sugar
110 g / 4 oz / ½ cup butter, softened
2 large eggs
1 lemon, zest finely grated

To decorate:

3 tbsp lemon curd
200 g / 7 oz / ⅔ cup ready-to-roll fondant icing
yellow food colouring
1–2 tsp lemon juice
150 g / 5 ½ oz / 1 ½ cups icing (confectioners') sugar
24 lemon jelly sweets

Lemon sweetie cupcakes

Method

STEP 1
Preheat the oven to 190°C (170°C fan) / 375F / gas 5 and line a 12-hole cupcake tin with paper cases.

STEP 2
Combine the flour, sugar, butter, eggs and lemon zest in a bowl and whisk together for 2 minutes or until smooth. Divide the mixture between the cases, then transfer the tin to the oven and bake for 10–15 minutes.

STEP 3
Test with a wooden toothpick, if it comes out clean, the cakes are done. Transfer the cakes to a wire rack and leave to cool completely.

STEP 4
Colour the fondant icing yellow, then roll it out and cut out 12 circles a little smaller in diameter than the top of the cakes. Spread the cakes with lemon curd, then smooth the icing on top.

STEP 5
Add a little lemon juice to the icing sugar, a few drops at a time, until it forms a smooth, spreadable icing. Spoon it into a piping bag fitted with a small plain nozzle and pipe a ring of dots around the outside of each cake. Use a blob of icing to secure two lemon jelly sweets in the centre of each cake.

Preparation time: **45 minutes** | Cooking time: **10–15 minutes** | Makes: **12**

Ingredients:

110 g / 4 oz / ⅔ cup self-raising flour, sifted
110 g / 4 oz / ½ cup caster (superfine) sugar
110 g / 4 oz / ½ cup butter, softened
1 tsp vanilla extract
2 large eggs

To decorate:

400 ml / 14 fl. oz / 1 ⅔ cups double (heavy) cream
4 tbsp caramel syrup

Caramel drizzle cupcakes

Method

STEP 1
Preheat the oven to 190°C (170°C fan) / 375F / gas 5 and line a 12-hole cupcake tin with paper cases.

STEP 2
Measure the cake ingredients into a bowl then whisk together for 3 minutes or until smooth and light. Divide the mixture between the paper cases, then transfer the tin to the oven and bake for 10–15 minutes.

STEP 3
Test the cakes with a toothpick; if it comes out clean, the cakes are done. Transfer the cakes to a wire rack and leave to cool completely.

STEP 4
Whip the cream until it holds its shape, then spoon it into a piping bag fitted with a large star nozzle and pipe a swirl on top of each cake. Drizzle over the caramel syrup.

Preparation time: 40 minutes | **Cooking time: 10–15 minutes** | **Makes: 12**

Ingredients:
110 g / 4 oz / ⅔ cup self-raising flour, sifted
110 g / 4 oz / ½ cup soft light brown sugar
110 g / 4 oz / ½ cup butter, softened
2 large eggs
1 tsp vanilla extract

To decorate:
110 g / 4 oz / ½ cup butter, softened
225 g / 8 oz / 2 ¼ cups icing (confectioners') sugar
2 tbsp milk
1 tsp vanilla extract
3 tbsp demerara sugar

Brown sugar cupcakes

Method

STEP 1
Preheat the oven to 190°C (170°C fan) / 375F / gas 5 and line a 12-hole cupcake tin with paper cases.

STEP 2
Combine the flour, sugar, butter, eggs and vanilla extract in a bowl and whisk together for 2 minutes or until smooth.

STEP 3
Divide the mixture between the cake cases then transfer the tin to the oven and bake for 10–15 minutes. Test with a wooden toothpick, if it comes out clean, the cakes are done. Transfer the cakes to a wire rack and leave to cool completely.

STEP 4
To make the buttercream, beat the butter until smooth then beat in the icing sugar. Use a whisk to incorporate the milk and vanilla extract, then whisk for 2 minutes or until well whipped.

STEP 5
Spread the buttercream onto the cakes and sprinkle with demerara sugar.

Preparation time: 45 minutes | **Cooking time: 10–15 minutes** | **Makes: 12**

Ingredients:

110 g / 4 oz / ⅔ cup self-raising flour, sifted
110 g / 4 oz / ½ cup caster (superfine) sugar
110 g / 4 oz / ½ cup butter, softened
2 large eggs
2 tbsp unsweetened cocoa powder

To decorate:

100 g / 3 ½ oz / ½ cup butter, softened
200 g / 7 oz / 2 cups icing (confectioners') sugar
100 g / 3 ½ oz / ⅓ cup blue or violet ready-to-roll fondant icing

Chocolate blossom cupcakes

Method

STEP 1
Preheat the oven to 190°C (170°C fan) / 375F / gas 5 and line a 12-hole cupcake tin with paper cases.

STEP 2
Combine the flour, sugar, butter, eggs and cocoa in a bowl and whisk together for 2 minutes or until smooth.

STEP 3
Divide the mixture between the cases, then transfer the tin to the oven and bake for 10–15 minutes. Test with a wooden toothpick, if it comes out clean, the cakes are done. Transfer the cakes to a wire rack and leave to cool completely.

STEP 4
Beat the butter until smooth, then gradually whisk in the icing sugar, adding a few drops of water if the mixture is too stiff.

STEP 5
Spoon the buttercream into a piping bag fitted with a large star nozzle and pipe a swirl onto each cake.

STEP 6
Roll out the fondant icing and use a small blossom plunger cutter to cut out the flowers. Arrange 3 flowers on top of each cake.

Preparation time: **1 hour 20 minutes** | Cooking time: **10–15 minutes** | Makes: **12**

Ingredients:

110 g / 4 oz / ⅔ cup self-raising flour, sifted
110 g / 4 oz / ½ cup caster (superfine) sugar
110 g / 4 oz / ½ cup butter, softened
2 large eggs
1 tsp vanilla extract
75 g / 2 ½ oz / ½ cup white chocolate chips

To decorate:

200 g / 7 oz / 1 ⅓ cups white chocolate
200 ml / 7 fl. oz / ¾ cup double (heavy) cream
12 jelly cherry sweets

White chocolate cherry cupcakes

Method

STEP 1

Preheat the oven to 190°C (170°C fan) / 375F / gas 5 and line a 12-hole cupcake tin with paper cases.

STEP 2

Combine the flour, sugar, butter, eggs and vanilla extract in a bowl and whisk together for 2 minutes or until smooth. Fold in the chocolate chips, then divide the mixture between the paper cases.

STEP 3

Transfer the tin to the oven and bake for 10–15 minutes. Test with a wooden toothpick, if it comes out clean, the cakes are done. Transfer the cakes to a wire rack and leave to cool completely.

STEP 4

Finely chop the chocolate and transfer it to a mixing bowl. Heat the cream until it starts to simmer, then pour it over the chocolate and leave to stand for 30 seconds. Slowly stir the chocolate and cream together until it forms a smooth ganache.

STEP 5

Leave the ganache to cool until it's thick enough to hold its shape, then spoon into a piping bag fitted with a medium star nozzle and pipe in a bow shape on top of the cakes. Decorate each one with a jelly cherry sweet.

Preparation time: **45 minutes** | Cooking time: **10–15 minutes** | Makes: **12**

Ingredients:

110 g / 4 oz / ⅔ cup self-raising flour, sifted
110 g / 4 oz / ½ cup caster (superfine) sugar
110 g / 4 oz / ½ cup butter, softened
1 tsp vanilla extract
2 large eggs

To decorate:

400 ml / 14 fl. oz / 1 ⅔ cups double (heavy) cream
3 large strawberries, sliced
1 kiwi, peeled, halved and sliced
6 seedless grapes, halved
36 blueberries
12 raspberries
icing (confectioners') sugar for dusting

Summer fruit cupcakes

Method

STEP 1
Preheat the oven to 190°C (170°C fan) / 375F / gas 5 and line a 12-hole cupcake tin with paper cases.

STEP 2
Measure the cake ingredients into a bowl then whisk together for 3 minutes or until smooth and light. Divide the mixture between the paper cases, then transfer the tin to the oven and bake for 10–15 minutes.

STEP 3
Test the cakes with a toothpick; if it comes out clean, the cakes are done. Transfer the cakes to a wire rack and leave to cool completely.

STEP 4
Whip the cream until it holds its shape, then spoon it into a piping bag fitted with a large star nozzle and pipe a swirl on top of each cake.

STEP 5
Arrange the fruit on top of the cakes and dust lightly with icing sugar.

Preparation time: 1 hour 20 minutes | **Cooking time: 10–15 minutes** | **Makes: 12**

Ingredients:

110 g / 4 oz / ⅔ cup self-raising flour, sifted
110 g / 4 oz / ½ cup caster (superfine) sugar
110 g / 4 oz / ½ cup butter, softened
2 large eggs
a few drops of peppermint essence
75 g / 2 ½ oz / ½ cup white chocolate chips

To decorate:

200 g / 7 oz / 1 ⅓ cups milk chocolate
200 ml / 7 fl. oz / ¾ cup double (heavy) cream
a few drops of peppermint essence
12 chocolate mint thins

Chocolate mint cream cupcakes

Method

STEP 1
Preheat the oven to 190°C (170°C fan) / 375F / gas 5 and line a 12-hole cupcake tin with paper cases.

STEP 2
Combine the flour, sugar, butter, eggs and peppermint essence in a bowl and whisk together for 2 minutes or until smooth. Fold in the chocolate chips, then divide the mixture between the paper cases.

STEP 3
Transfer the tin to the oven and bake for 10–15 minutes. Test with a wooden toothpick, if it comes out clean, the cakes are done. Transfer the cakes to a wire rack and leave to cool completely.

STEP 4
Finely chop the chocolate and transfer it to a mixing bowl. Heat the cream until it starts to simmer, then pour it over the chocolate and leave to stand for 30 seconds. Slowly stir the chocolate and cream together with the peppermint essence until it forms a smooth ganache.

STEP 5
Leave the ganache to cool until it's thick enough to hold its shape, then spoon it into a piping bag fitted with a large plain nozzle. Pipe a swirl of ganache onto each cake and top with the mint thins.

Preparation time: **45 minutes** | Cooking time: **10–15 minutes** | Makes: **12**

Ingredients:
110 g / 4 oz / ⅔ cup self-raising flour, sifted
110 g / 4 oz / ½ cup caster (superfine) sugar
110 g / 4 oz / ½ cup butter, softened
1 lemon, zest finely grated
2 large eggs

To decorate:
4 tbsp passion fruit curd
400 ml / 14 fl. oz / 1 ⅔ cups double (heavy) cream
4 passion fruit

Passion fruit cream cupcakes

Method

STEP 1
Preheat the oven to 190°C (170°C fan) / 375F / gas 5 and line a 12-hole cupcake tin with paper cases.

STEP 2
Measure the cake ingredients into a bowl then whisk together for 3 minutes or until smooth and light. Divide the mixture between the paper cases, then transfer the tin to the oven and bake for 10–15 minutes.

STEP 3
Test the cakes with a toothpick; if it comes out clean, the cakes are done. Transfer the cakes to a wire rack and leave to cool completely.

STEP 4
Cut a cone out of the centre of each cake and fill it with passion fruit curd before replacing the cake.

STEP 5
Whip the cream until it holds its shape, then spread a third of it over the cakes. Spoon the rest into a piping bag fitted with a large star nozzle and pipe a ring on top of each cake.

STEP 6
Cut the passion fruit in half and scrape out the pulp and seeds, then spoon them into the centre.

Preparation time: **45 minutes** | Cooking time: **10–15 minutes** | Makes: **12**

Ingredients:

110 g / 4 oz / ⅔ cup self-raising flour, sifted
110 g / 4 oz / ½ cup caster (superfine) sugar
110 g / 4 oz / ½ cup butter, softened
2 large eggs
1 tsp vanilla extract

To decorate:

3 tbsp morello cherry jam (jelly)
110 g / 4 oz / ½ cup butter, softened
225 g / 8 oz / 2 ¼ cups icing (confectioners') sugar
1 tsp vanilla extract
sugar confetti for sprinkling
12 fresh cherries
12 fondant waffers

Cherry and vanilla cupcakes

Method

STEP 1
Preheat the oven to 190°C (170°C fan) / 375F / gas 5 and line a 12-hole cupcake tin with paper cases.

STEP 2
Combine the flour, sugar, butter, eggs and vanilla extract in a bowl and whisk together for 2 minutes or until smooth.

STEP 3
Divide the mixture between the cake cases then transfer the tin to the oven and bake for 10–15 minutes. Test with a wooden toothpick, if it comes out clean, the cakes are done. Transfer the cakes to a wire rack and leave to cool completely.

STEP 4
Cut a cone out of the centre of each cake and fill with the jam, before replacing the cake.

STEP 5
To make the buttercream, beat the butter until smooth then beat in the icing sugar and vanilla extract. Spread a third of the icing over the top of the cakes.

STEP 6
Spoon the rest of the buttercream into a piping bag fitted with a large star nozzle and pipe a swirl on top of each cake. Sprinkle with sugar confetti and top each one with a cherry and a fondant wafer.

Preparation time: 50 minutes | **Cooking time: 10–15 minutes** | **Makes: 12**

Ingredients:

110 g / 4 oz / ⅔ cup self-raising flour, sifted
110 g / 4 oz / ½ cup caster (superfine) sugar
110 g / 4 oz / ½ cup butter, softened
2 large eggs
1 tsp vanilla extract
75 g / 2 ½ oz / ½ cup white chocolate chips

To decorate:

300 ml / 10 ½ fl. oz / 1 ¼ cups double (heavy) cream
white chocolate vermicelli to sprinkle
12 chocolate cookies
100 g / 3 ½ oz / ⅔ cups dark chocolate (minimum 60% cocoa solids)

Chocolate cookie cupcakes

Method

STEP 1
Preheat the oven to 190°C (170°C fan) / 375F / gas 5 and line a 12-hole cupcake tin with paper cases.

STEP 2
Combine the flour, sugar, butter, eggs and vanilla extract in a bowl and whisk together for 2 minutes or until smooth. Fold in the chocolate chips, then divide the mixture between the paper cases.

STEP 3
Transfer the tin to the oven and bake for 10–15 minutes. Test with a wooden toothpick, if it comes out clean, the cakes are done. Transfer the cakes to a wire rack and leave to cool completely.

STEP 4
Whip the cream until it holds its shape, then spoon it into a piping bag fitted with a large star nozzle and pipe a swirl on top of each cake. Sprinkle with white chocolate vermicelli.

STEP 5
Insert a cookie into the top of each cake, then melt the dark chocolate and drizzle it over the top.

Preparation time: **45 minutes** | Cooking time: **10–15 minutes** | Makes: **11**

Ingredients:
110 g / 4 oz / ⅔ cup self-raising flour, sifted
110 g / 4 oz / ½ cup caster (superfine) sugar
110 g / 4 oz / ½ cup butter, softened
2 large eggs
2 tbsp unsweetened cocoa powder

To decorate:
100 g / 3 ½ oz / ½ cup butter, softened
200 g / 7 oz / 2 cups icing (confectioners') sugar
1 tsp vanilla extract

Cake crumb cupcakes

Method

STEP 1
Preheat the oven to 190°C (170°C fan) / 375F / gas 5 and line a 12-hole cupcake tin with paper cases.

STEP 2
Combine the flour, sugar, butter, eggs and cocoa in a bowl and whisk together for 2 minutes or until smooth.

STEP 3
Divide the mixture between the cases, then transfer the tin to the oven and bake for 10–15 minutes. Test with a wooden toothpick, if it comes out clean, the cakes are done. Transfer the cakes to a wire rack and leave to cool completely.

STEP 4
Beat the butter until smooth, then gradually whisk in the icing sugar and vanilla extract.

STEP 5
Spoon the buttercream into a piping bag fitted with a large star nozzle and pipe it onto 11 of the cupcakes. Crumble up the twelfth cupcake and sprinkle it over the top of the others.

Preparation time: **40 minutes** | Cooking time: **10–15 minutes** | Makes: **12**

Ingredients:
110 g / 4 oz / ⅔ cup self-raising flour, sifted
110 g / 4 oz / ½ cup caster (superfine) sugar
110 g / 4 oz / ½ cup butter, softened
2 large eggs
1 tsp vanilla extract

To decorate:
110 g / 4 oz / ½ cup butter, softened
225 g / 8 oz / 2 ¼ cups icing (confectioners') sugar, plus extra for dusting
2 tbsp milk
1 tsp vanilla extract
12 chocolate cream cookies

Chocolate cream cookie cupcakes

Method

STEP 1
Preheat the oven to 190°C (170°C fan) / 375F / gas 5 and line a 12-hole cupcake tin with paper cases.

STEP 2
Combine the flour, sugar, butter, eggs and vanilla extract in a bowl and whisk together for 2 minutes or until smooth.

STEP 3
Divide the mixture between the cake cases then transfer the tin to the oven and bake for 10–15 minutes. Test with a wooden toothpick, if it comes out clean, the cakes are done. Transfer the cakes to a wire rack and leave to cool completely.

STEP 4
To make the buttercream, beat the butter until smooth then beat in the icing sugar. Use a whisk to incorporate the milk and vanilla extract, then whisk for 2 minutes or until well whipped.

STEP 5
Cut 6 of the chocolate cream cookies in half and reserve for decoration then finely chop the rest. Fold the cookie pieces into the buttercream and spoon it onto the cakes. Top each cake with half a cookie.

Preparation time: **40 minutes** | Cooking time: **10–15 minutes** | Makes: **12**

Ingredients:

110 g / 4 oz / ⅔ cup self-raising flour, sifted
110 g / 4 oz / ½ cup caster (superfine) sugar
110 g / 4 oz / ½ cup butter, softened
2 large eggs
1 tbsp matcha green tea powder

To decorate:

110 g / 4 oz / ½ cup butter, softened
225 g / 8 oz / 2 ¼ cups icing (confectioners') sugar, plus extra for dusting
a few drops of green food colouring
12 green seedless grapes

Grape and green tea cupcakes

Method

STEP 1
Preheat the oven to 190°C (170°C fan) / 375F / gas 5 and line a 12-hole cupcake tin with paper cases.

STEP 2
Combine the flour, sugar, butter, eggs and matcha powder in a bowl and whisk together for 2 minutes or until smooth.

STEP 3
Divide the mixture between the cake cases then transfer the tin to the oven and bake for 10–15 minutes. Test with a wooden toothpick, if it comes out clean, the cakes are done. Transfer the cakes to a wire rack and leave to cool completely.

STEP 4
To make the buttercream, beat the butter until smooth then beat in the icing sugar. Divide the buttercream into 2 bowls and colour 1 bowl pale green, then ripple them together and spoon onto the cakes.

STEP 5
Top each cake with a grape.

Preparation time: **40 minutes** | Cooking time: **10–15 minutes** | Makes: **12**

Ingredients:
110 g / 4 oz / ⅔ cup self-raising flour, sifted
110 g / 4 oz / ½ cup caster (superfine) sugar
110 g / 4 oz / ½ cup butter, softened
2 large eggs
1 large banana, finely chopped

To decorate:
200 g / 7 oz / ⅔ cup dulce de leche
2 bananas, sliced
300 ml / 10 ½ fl. oz / 1 ¼ cups double (heavy) cream
2 tbsp milk chocolate curls

Banoffee cupcakes

Method

STEP 1
Preheat the oven to 190°C (170°C fan) / 375F / gas 5 and line a 12-hole cupcake tin with paper cases.

STEP 2
Measure the cake ingredients into a bowl then whisk together for 3 minutes or until smooth and light. Divide the mixture between the paper cases and bake for 10–15 minutes or until a skewer inserted comes out clean. Leave to cool completely.

STEP 3
Spoon the dulce de leche onto the cakes and spread it out with the back of the spoon. Reserve 12 banana slices and layer the rest on top of the dulce de leche.

STEP 4
Whip the cream until it holds its shape, then pipe a swirl on top of each cake. Top with the reserved banana slices and sprinkle with chocolate curls.

Index